THE
MIRACLE
METHOD

Working with the Problem Drinker

THE
MIRACLE
METHOD

*A RADICALLY NEW APPROACH
TO PROBLEM DRINKING*

————————☐————————

SCOTT D. MILLER, PH.D.
INSOO KIM BERG, MSSW

W. W. NORTON & COMPANY ☐ NEW YORK / LONDON

Library of Congress Catalog Card No. 95-162277

The text and display of this book are set in New Caledonia. Composition
and manufacturing by the Haddon Craftsmen, Inc. Book design by Roberta
Flechner

ISBN 0-393-31533-9

W. W. Norton & Company, Inc., 500 Fifth Avenue, New York, N.Y. 10110
W. W. Norton & Company Ltd., 10 Coptic Street, London WC1A 1PU

1 2 3 4 5 6 7 8 9 0

To my parents, Paul and Darlene Miller, whose relationship first taught me to believe in miracles, and to my dear wife, Dr. Karen M. Donahey, who turned that belief into reality.

S. D. M.

To all of the problem drinkers who taught me how to listen.

I. K. B.

Contents

Acknowledgments

A great deal of gratitude is owed to the many people who have contributed to our thinking, research, and writing over the years. First, however, we want to thank those clients with whom we have worked over the last twenty-odd years. Our interactions with you afforded us the possibility of sharing your hopes and dreams for a better future. Those dreams in turn inspired us to work hard to understand the source of your hope, while simultaneously challenging us to open our minds to new ways of thinking about and understanding the change process. We trust that this book accurately reflects the faith you have taught us to have in the human potential for growth and change.

Special thanks go to the many colleagues and friends who have played a role in shaping the ideas we present in the book. We are indebted to you for listening to us, challenging our thinking, telling us we were wrong, and sticking by us as our thinking has evolved. You are simply too numerous to mention. Please know, however, that your participation in our workshops, training seminars, and supervision hours has challenged and stimulated our thinking and that the experience you have shared with us is represented in the ideas contained in this book. (All this times two if you happen to live in Virginia!)

We want to thank by name a number of our colleagues who have both mentored and expanded our clinical work with their professional example, including Larry Hopwood, Lynn D. Johnson, Bill O'Hanlon, Jeffrey K. Zeig, Michelle Weiner-Davis, John Weakland, Harold Miller, Jr., Steve de Shazer, Jane Kashnig, John Walters, and Jane Peller.

Finally, a great deal of gratitude is owed our editor, Susan Barrows Munro, who encouraged us to broaden our horizons by writing a self-help book and was patient during the many changes that occurred during the process.

Preface

Nothing is as dangerous as an idea when it is the
only one you have.

—Émile Chartier

A picture held us captive.

—Ludwig Wittgenstein, *Philosophical
Investigations*

Sometime ago now the two of us met during a workshop on
the treatment of people with drinking problems. Over the
course of the three-day training we talked about our experiences
treating people who were having problems as a result of their
own or another person's drinking. We also shared some surprisingly similar professional and personal experiences.

Insoo, Scott learned, had grown up in Korea during the
height of the Korean conflict, living with her family in a small
village. During that turbulent and violent time, she recalled,
many villagers coped with the war by what she and others referred to as "drinking too much." At the time no one labeled
these village drinkers "alcoholic" or even "problem drinkers."

On one of the walks Scott and Insoo took during that three-
day training, Scott learned that one of the village members who
happened to "drink too much" was Insoo's father. He had been
a quiet, thoughtful scholar and a gentle man. But the combination of the war and alcohol eventually changed him into a bois-
terous, loud, and at times physically abusive man. Insoo remembered many times having to clean up her father and put him to
bed after a drinking episode. The next day, of course, nothing
was said.

Insoo's openness and obviously heartfelt feelings about her

father's drinking led Scott to share how alcohol had affected his own family. Scott's uncle, Insoo learned, began drinking to "calm his nerves" during his tour of duty as a radio officer in World War II. Scott related how the military leaders had actually encouraged their troops to drink and supplied the battle-weary soldiers with alcohol as a way of coping with the horrors of war. Alcohol was not the only substance that his uncle began to use while in the service. Although he came from a family and religious background that prohibited the use of tobacco, Scott's uncle began smoking while he was a soldier. When he left the service, he was smoking three and a half packages of cigarettes a day.

In the years following his discharge from the service, Scott's uncle continued to use alcohol. Friends expressed concern, and family members offered to help. They even pleaded with him to change—all to no avail. His problems with alcohol ultimately resulted in the loss of his career and family. In addition, despite warnings from his doctor that he was developing emphysema and a serious circulatory problem, he continued to smoke heavily.

After the Korean War Insoo moved to the United States and, as part of her training as a therapist, began learning about the treatment of persons with alcohol problems. She quickly realized that many of the people in her village, including her father, had been more than simply "drinking too much." She recognized that her father could easily have been labeled an "alcoholic" or, at the very least, an "alcohol abuser" or "dependent." In the training programs about alcohol treatment, she learned that there was only "one way" for people like her father to be helped, and that was to join Alcoholics Anonymous (AA), admit that they were powerless over alcohol, turn their lives over to a "higher power," and follow the AA Twelve Steps for the remainder of their lives. To do otherwise could result in only one thing: the continued progression of the disease and eventual death.

Scott had received similar training. To support himself in

graduate school, he accepted a job as an alcohol counselor—a job his professors considered beneath the dignity of a psychologist in training. To prepare him to work the "right way" with people having alcohol problems, the agency he worked for sent him to numerous training programs. At the time his uncle was still drinking and smoking despite his many personal losses and the deterioration of his physical health. According to the instruction Scott was receiving, his uncle's drinking was due to the fact that he had a disease and that he was in denial. Scott learned that what members of his family would say were their repeated and benevolently motivated attempts to help their ailing loved one was actually perpetuating the problem by "enabling" his uncle's drinking.

At some point during one of our conversations at that three-day workshop, one of us, although we don't recall which, asked the other what eventually happened to the loved one with the alcohol problem. To our mutual surprise, neither of them drank himself to death! To the contrary, each of our respective family members eventually discontinued his use of alcohol. Moreover, neither one had resorted to getting any formal treatment or to attending AA meetings. Neither of us could recall any fuss, any dramatic moment or turning point, and we certainly could not recall either of our relatives' "hitting bottom" or turning his life over to a "higher power."

For both of us, trained in the traditional model of alcohol treatment, this seemed impossible. It had been drilled into our heads that no one who has the "disease of alcoholism" can stop drinking without treatment. Indeed, at one time or another in our careers both of us had read what Vernon Johnson, one of the leading authorities in the field, had written on this very topic. A typical example: "Unless the chemically dependent person gets help, he or she *will* die prematurely. . . . Chemical dependency is . . . progressive . . . [and] this means that it *always* gets worse if left untreated."[1] Perhaps, we both reasoned initially, our relatives were simply not *real* alcoholics or, in Johnson's words, "chemically dependent." However, we both had abandoned this thought long ago, given the chronic nature of our relatives' problems and the very real pain that alcohol had caused our families. If any persons fitted the picture of "alcoholic," they certainly were our relatives.

To complicate matters further, Insoo related that her father had continued to drink socially throughout the remainder of his long life. This, we agreed, was supposed to be impossible since, as Johnson also pointed out, "once a person becomes chemically dependent, he or she remains so *forever.*"[2] No one was supposed to be able to drink normally if he or she had "the disease," yet Insoo's father had somehow "disciplined" himself to drink socially despite his years of abuse. Moreover, no one was supposed to be able to stop drinking without treatment, yet both Insoo's father and Scott's uncle had done exactly that: quit without any formal or informal treatment! Additionally, Scott's uncle quit smoking the same day he quit drinking.

After reflecting on the apparent contradiction between our clinical training and the experiences of our relatives, Scott asked Insoo if she had any ideas about how her father had actually managed to change his drinking. She said that she had wondered about this before—in particular when she was going through alcoholism treatment training—but that she really had no idea how her father had managed to change his drinking. Scott responded similarly when Insoo asked the same question about his uncle. One Mother's Day, Scott remembered, his uncle simply announced that he was no longer going to drink or smoke. Although no one in the family was convinced, he did indeed stop cold.

In short, we had to conclude that neither of us had any real idea about how our relatives had managed to stop their drinking. They just simply seemed to go from having a serious drinking problem one day to not having that problem the next day. Both of them had somehow accomplished the theoretically impossible.

That neither of us had any idea how our relatives had managed this theoretically impossible event was a sobering realization. We had not thought much about it at the time, and our training had led us to believe that these truly miraculous changes had little to teach us about recovering from serious alcohol problems. What was important, we had learned, was recognizing the signs and symptoms of "the disease," confronting denial, and helping people get connected to the "right" way of dealing with alcohol problems: lifelong participation in a recovery program. In other words, we had learned that nothing of value could be learned from the successes of our two relatives. Not only that, but we had, in fact, learned that their successes were impossible!

The cost of such thinking is clear. Pledging allegiance to a theory had actually led us to ignore the ways in which our relatives changed their lives. In other words, we missed a golden opportunity to learn something valuable about solving serious alcohol problems from two successful people. How had they done it? What had they done anyway? Given that both were dead, we simply had to accept the fact that we would never know. What was worse, however, was recognizing how the strong, nearly totalitarian allegiance to a single theory and method of treatment was leading the field of alcohol treatment to continue to miss the same opportunity.

Our conversation continued. Each of us, we admitted, had long questioned some of the central tenets of the traditional treatment philosophy. Insoo related the first time she was really confronted with a situation that just did not seem to fit with her training, an experience with an old friend, "Bob."

Bob was a good friend who happened to be a twenty-five-year recovering alcoholic. Insoo said there was nothing that unusual about Bob except that he was a Lutheran minister who, as part of his official duties, offered communion every Sunday of the year, communion that, Insoo was surprised to learn, Pastor Bob ministered with wine—real wine! Each Sunday for the last twenty-five years Bob had stood before the congregation and served himself and then his parishioners wine as part of the official sacraments of the church.

Insoo recalled struggling with what she had been taught in school about people who were "recovering" from alcohol problems. In particular, these people were *not* supposed to be able to manage drinking alcoholic beverages—however small—without triggering a craving for more alcohol, which would eventually lead to a relapse. Remember the old AA slogan: Problem drinkers are always "One drink away from a drunk!" To this end Insoo related how she had once confronted her clients and, as indicated in the *Big Book* of AA, urged them to "admit they were powerless over alcohol."[3] Her experience with Bob, however, led her to question some of her cherished beliefs about alcohol. This questioning eventually led her to experiment with new and different treatment methods, methods which, she told Scott, she at first kept secret from her friends and professional colleagues.

Keeping a secret was a situation Scott could identify with. Working with chronic problem drinkers in a public agency, he found that the methods he had learned in his traditional training did not seem to work very often. For one thing, from 30 to 60 percent of the clients dropped out of the treatment programs after only a few sessions—victims, he was told, of the insidious disease of alcoholism. Being able to "blame" treatment failures on the disease of alcoholism, however, offered little solace. Early on Scott began to wonder if there wasn't some way to keep in treatment those who obviously needed help. He told Insoo how he had secretly sought out supervision in other treatment models and begun incorporating different methods into his work with problem drinkers. Abandoning a central tenet of the traditional treatment model, Scott gave up the idea of lifelong recovery and started seeing clients with alcohol problems for a limited number of sessions.

Insoo then told how her subsequent work with Vietnam veterans and homeless problem drinkers led her, together with a team of therapists, to begin formulating an alternative to the traditional treatment model. Eventually she gained the confidence to share some of her ideas with other treatment professionals. In turn, Scott related how he, in another part of the country, had also been putting together various alternative approaches that he was now beginning to share with other professionals.

On the last day of the workshop both of us decided to "stay in contact." As we corresponded over the next few years, we exchanged ideas, and slowly a coherent approach began to take shape. Eventually we decided that we needed to be geographically closer in order to continue our work, so Scott relocated to the Midwest.

Together we have now interviewed and worked with hundreds and hundreds of clients who have alcohol problems. For the most part our work has been organized around a very simple idea: identifying how those clients who successfully overcome their problems with alcohol are able to do so. As a result, we have developed a method for dealing with alcohol problems that is based on what we have learned from our successful clients. This approach has been applied to all types of clients: mild to serious alcohol problems in people from a variety of social, economic, racial, cultural, and family backgrounds. We have come to expect that success is not only a theoretical possibility but also a practical reality.

In an earlier book, *Working with the Problem Drinker,* we described this method, which has been called the solution-focused approach, to an audience of professional counselors and therapists. We are pleased that that book, despite—or perhaps because of—the rather heretical ideas contained in it, has generated considerable excitement among treatment professionals. Like us, they have not found the "one-size-fits-all" approach of the traditional treatment model helpful for treating the increasingly diverse numbers of people with alcohol problems. We are not the only professionals pursuing this approach to treating alcohol problems. Indeed, a considerable amount of research and thinking is being done that closely parallels our own work. In this book we will draw on others' work to illustrate various points and to add depth and perspective to our own work.

Our hope is that the reader, rather than having to learn the hard way, as we did, can benefit from our experience and the experience of the many clients we have been privileged to work with and learn from over the last several years.

1

The Miracle Method

HELP AND HOPE FOR THE
PROBLEM DRINKER

> They say miracles are past.
> —William Shakespeare, *All's Well That Ends Well*

> "There's no use trying," she [Alice] said: "one *can't* believe impossible things."
> "I daresay you haven't had much practice," said the Queen. "When I was your age, I always did it for half-an-hour a day. Why, sometimes I've believed as many as six impossible things before breakfast."
> —Lewis Carroll, *Through the Looking Glass*

You did it! You have picked up a book that describes a method that has been used successfully in the United States and abroad to help thousands of people overcome their problems with alcohol. A method which offers hope in addition to practical, step-by-step, here-is-how-to-do-it advice for beating your difficulties with alcohol. A method which, by the way, does not require a lifelong commitment to some type of program or set of beliefs in order to be successful. You can *start* changing today and be making the progress you desire at the pace that feels comfortable to you simply by continuing to read this book.

You will not be asked to turn your entire life upside down or inside out or to go on a psychoarchaeology expedition back to your childhood to discover and piece together the various elements of your life that may be causing your problem. Neither will you be asked to turn your life over to some expert, authority or "higher power" outside yourself. You won't even be asked to promise that you will never to drink again. You will simply be helped to discover the resources and strengths that you possess right now that can be used to bring about the changes you desire. That is what the miracle method is all about: *rallying your own strengths and resources in order to solve your problems with alcohol.*

Now we know that like Alice in Wonderland, you may find it impossible to believe that a self-help book could ever solve a problem that is as serious and beguiling as problem drinking seems to be, much less a self-help book entitled *The Miracle Method.* With such a bold title you may be wondering what we are promising and if we can deliver. Perhaps you have already read several books from the recovery section of your local bookstore or attended meetings of one or more of the ever-growing number of self-help groups aimed at people with drinking problems. Maybe you've been through one of those inpatient treatment programs. You know the type: the ones with the flashy and moving television ads. "Call now. We can help! We *promise.*"

You may even be in some sort of treatment as you read these paragraphs. They all make promises. You may have found, however, that the promises made in the recovery books, in the treatment programs, and by the various alcoholism treatment experts don't exactly square with reality. "The ideas sound real good," a client of ours once said, "when you read about them in a book. It's only when you try to apply them in your life that all the difficulties start." What's to say, then, that this book is any different from what you have already tried or may be trying now? Well, read on and see.

WARNING!

The miracle method will definitely challenge your thinking about how to solve problems. You will not be able to think about your problem and its solution in the way that you did before reading this book.

We tell you this up front so that you can save your money if you are one of those people who insist on thinking about and seeing things in a certain way. If nothing else, the miracle method will challenge your thinking about how alcohol problems can be solved. In fact, part of the miracle of this method involves challenging you to think differently so that you can stop using those problem-solving strategies that not only are *not* helping but may actually be perpetuating your problems with alcohol. That's right. You didn't misread. Quite often our attempts to solve our problems keep those problems from being solved. Somehow we get tricked into repeating more of the same strategy or thinking about how to solve a problem even though that thinking and strategy have not produced the result we desire or have even made the problem worse.

A practical example of this is what happens when we look for a lost object. Think about the last time you were looking for something you had misplaced. First, you try to think about when you had the object last. Then you retrace your steps, looking for the object at each place along the way. Your frustration grows as you go from place to place, trying to locate the object without success. What do you do when you have finally exhausted all the places to look for the object? Look somewhere else? Try something different? Usually not. If you are like most people, you start looking in the same places all over again!

This reminds us of an old story about a man named Steve who was taking a leisurely stroll down the street one bright, sunny afternoon. Out of the corner of his eye he noticed a man on the opposite side of the street who was obviously trying to get his attention. Steve stopped and acknowledged the man, who quickly crossed the street and, approaching Steve, proclaimed loudly, "My God! It is you! I knew it was, I would know you anywhere." The man stretched out his hand and added, "How good to see you!" Steve did not recognize the man, who seemed to be treating him like some long-lost relative or friend. Not wanting to offend the person, however, Steve simply nodded, deciding to play along until he could perhaps figure out the man's identity.

The man continued, shaking his head from side to side. "My goodness, how long has it been?"

Steve, still buying time, simply raised his eyebrows and looked away.

"Ten? Fifteen years?" the man then asked, only to follow quickly with "You have really changed!"

Steve simply nodded.

Reaching out and patting Steve on the stomach, the man said, "Why, look at you! You've put on weight." Steve, who was trying desperately to locate this man in his memory, was taken somewhat aback by this comment; after all, he had always been a little chunky. But before he could say anything, the man added, "And your hair, why, you have changed that, too! So you are a blond now, eh?"

This comment really surprised Steve, who was born a towhead and had never changed his hair color. Perhaps, he thought, the man, whom he still could not remember, simply had forgotten this trivial detail. "Well"—the man quickly went on, slapping Steve on the shoulder and speaking in a feigned whisper—"you know what they say, huh? Blondes have more fun! I guess that holds for men, too!"

Steve smiled, still racking his brain.

Then, inching closer and peering into Steve's eyes, the man began laughing out loud and said, "Why, your eyes are brown now. You've even changed your eye color. You crazy guy! You have changed almost everything about yourself, Jack!"

"Jack?" Steve said, speaking for the first time during the whole encounter. "My name is *not* Jack! My name is Steve!"

"Why, Jack," the man said, not missing a beat, "you've even changed your name!"

Like the gentleman in the story, you can easily get stuck repeating the same strategy even when it is not working. The "miracle" method will challenge you to think differently and to try some other strategies to solve your drinking problem. While it will be difficult at times to have your thinking challenged, it is the only way we know to stimulate your creativity and empower you to try something different. Different enough, in other words, to enable you to take control over alcohol rather than have alcohol remain in control of you. The process will require some work on your part, but the results will be worth it. If you are willing to have your thinking challenged and to experiment with something totally different, then read on.

WARNING!

You will have to use your imagination *for a change.*

Following the guidelines set forth in the pages of this book will also require you to use your imagination to bring about the changes you desire. You will have to use your brain if you want to achieve the miracle that this method promises to deliver. There's simply no getting by this requirement. This doesn't mean that you have to be a genius; however, you *will* have to play an active part in making the method work for you. We are unable, nor would we see it preferable, simply to pour a one-size-fits-all method for solving alcohol problems into your head.

Indeed, as you will read in the next chapter, we believe that the one-size-fits-all mentality that characterizes current approaches to problem drinking has severely limited the options available to people struggling to overcome problems with alcohol. The limited number of treatment options has led many problem drinkers to believe that there is no hope for recovery if they have failed these traditional treatments. Nothing could be further from the truth. There is hope and help available.

Together with your imagination, the miracle method will help you develop your own personal strategy for winning the battle against booze. Indeed, this may be one of the only approaches for helping problem drinkers that use their creative abilities to develop individualized plans for recovery. If you can suspend your disbelief long enough to try out a different way of thinking about and solving your problem, then read on.

WHAT IF NOTHING ELSE HAS WORKED?

"What if nothing else has worked?" you may ask. "Can the miracle method even help me?" We know that it can be very discouraging to have tried and failed to overcome an alcohol problem. Please know, however, that you are not alone. Many problem drinkers—the majority, in fact—experience some degree of failure while trying to find a strategy that works for them. Can the miracle method help you? The answer is an unqualified yes. Even if you are a problem drinker who has been labeled a "chronic relapser"—someone who constantly falls off the wagon—the method can be helpful. Even if you have been through several traditional treatment programs and failed them all, the method can be helpful. What is critical in all such instances is to try something different. Believe us, the miracle method will be different.

WHAT IF I DON'T THINK I HAVE AN
ALCOHOL PROBLEM?

Perhaps you are not reading this book because you think you have a problem with alcohol. Maybe you are one of those people who are reading this book because someone close to you—your spouse, a parent, a child—thinks that you have a problem with alcohol. Maybe you are reading this book as part of a treatment program that you have been forced to attend. Your view, perhaps, is that you are in treatment because you were in the wrong place at the wrong time. For example, you may have been arrested for driving under the influence of alcohol or for public intoxication. You may think that testing fate—not your use of alcohol—proved your undoing. Being in treatment is not your idea. Your view of the situation is that *others* are your biggest problem. Your spouse is nagging you; your employer is making threats; the judge is giving you a choice between jail or treatment. Can the method described in this book help in these kinds of circumstances? What if you don't even think you have an alcohol problem?

Believe it or not, the method described in this book can help. By following the method, you will be helped to develop some successful strategies for dealing with the people who are complaining about your behavior. Most of our experience has been in working with people who have been under some type of external pressure to be in treatment. Either the judge has sent them or treatment is part of their probation or parole agreements. At minimum, most of our clients have family members who complain about their drinking. Our experience has taught us something that you may already know—that is, simply biding time in some kind of treatment program will probably not be enough to satisfy the people who complain about you. These people want results. They will probably not stop complaining until they see some evidence that you are at least trying. You can use the method to help yourself out of this situation and meet the de-

mands of others while simultaneously maintaining your dignity
and independence.

WHAT IF SOMEONE ELSE HAS THE PROBLEM?

The method can also be helpful if you happen to be on the other
side of a drinking problem. Perhaps you are a family member or
the spouse of a problem drinker. Maybe you have a close friend,
employee, or colleague who has a problem with alcohol. As you
probably know or have learned from experience, coaxing the
problem drinker to seek help is a frustrating experience with
limited success. Too often such coaxing serves only to strain and
even to break a relationship. Watching a problem drinker slowly
die or destroy those around him or her is not an acceptable alternative either. Following the ideas suggested in this book can be
helpful in developing a plan to help the problem drinker as well
as yourself. If you are prepared to give the method a try, then
read on.

HOW TO GET THE MOST OUT OF THE
MIRACLE METHOD

In the coming pages we will introduce you to the miracle
method. Each chapter in the book explains some particular aspect of the method and provides you with step-by-step instructions for applying that aspect to your problem. Later chapters
build on the principles and strategies explained in earlier chapters. For this reason it is best to read the chapters in order. Stories, case examples, and excerpts of dialogue from our own work
with problem drinkers are used throughout the book to high-
light and clarify important points as well as to help you apply the
ideas to your own personal situation. You might find it useful to
have a notebook nearby while you read the book in order to

write down and keep track of the ideas that occur to you and the strategies that are suggested. As you read the book and try to apply the ideas to your own personal situation, pay close attention to those suggestions and recommendations you find most helpful—in other words, those ideas that help you achieve your desired objective. Then—and this is important—once you find something that makes sense and works for you, *keep doing it!* At the same time, please don't feel as if you must follow every suggestion in the book in order to be successful. In your reading, you are bound to come across some ideas that are not helpful or that do not fit with your personal situation or experience. Keep these ideas in the back of your head for future reference or toss them out completely. The important thing is not to follow the program we have found but to find a program that you can follow.

You can begin making the miracle method work in your life by turning to the next chapter, where we set the stage for using the method successfully by describing the basic principles and assumptions of the approach. Good luck, and remember to have fun along the way.

2

Therapist-Dependent No More!

THE SOLUTION REVOLUTION IN SUBSTANCE ABUSE AND MENTAL HEALTH TREATMENT

> When I focus on what's good today, I have a good day, and when I focus on what's bad, I have a bad day. *If I focus on a problem, the problem increases; if I focus on the answer, the answer increases.*
> —Alcoholics Anonymous, *The Big Book*

> Well, darkness has a hunger that's insatiable, and lightness has a call that's hard to hear.
> —Emily Saliers, "Closer to Fine"

$\mathbf{A}$ few years ago we showed a videotape of a family we had interviewed to a group of therapists we were training. Following the hourlong tape, we asked the therapists to use their skills to describe what they had observed. They quickly began describing the family and its various members. The mother, the therapists agreed, was obviously an "angry and controlling woman" who was frustrated with her marriage and overwhelmed by her child-rearing responsibilities. However, her "outward" expression of anger was really, the therapists told us, only the superficial manifestation of an "underlying" depression. On the other hand, the woman's husband and the father of their three children was described as "cut-off, distant, and even alienated" from the rest of the family. A few of the therapists, with backgrounds in chemical dependency and addiction treatment, used their expertise to identify the signs of what they believed was a "hidden" drinking problem in the father. In particular, these therapists pointed out the way in which the wife consistently "enabled" the man to remain aloof with her and the children during the interview. Others pointed to certain aspects of the interaction between the father and his eight-year-old daughter and speculated that he might be sexually abusing her.

After a while we asked what they thought should be done with the family. They had many suggestions. First, all the therapists agreed that the family should continue with some sort of family therapy at our clinic. In addition, the therapists thought that the woman should be referred to a psychiatrist for evaluation and possible medical treatment of the chemical imbalance that was causing the underlying depression they had observed. The alcohol counselors in the group recommended that the father be referred to an addiction specialist. Only such a person, they assured us, would have the requisite knowledge for dealing with the denial that always seems to accompany people with drinking problems. This denial, they observed, was obviously responsible for the problems they had seen on the videotape. Finally, several suggested that we interview the eight-year-old daughter separately in order to investigate the possibility of sexual abuse by her "alcoholic" father.

Once the therapists had finished with their descriptions and recommendations, we informed them that the mother, father, and daughter seen on the videotape were not really clients at all and actually never had been. Instead, the family had been part of an experiment designed to teach therapists how their beliefs bias what they see in their clinical work with individuals and families. Far from being sick, we assured the group, the individuals on the tape constituted a healthy and well-functioning family who happened to live in our neighborhood and were longtime friends! Not a single one of their therapeutic opinions, the members of the group were surprised to learn, had been correct.

THE PROBLEM FOCUS OF TRADITIONAL TREATMENT

We conducted our little experiment several times and obtained largely the same results on each occasion. At no time did any of therapists who participated describe any signs of mental health. To the contrary, while the problems that were identified differed from one training group to the next, the family was always viewed as "sick" and in need of treatment. Despite having been aware of other researchers who had conducted the same experiment and obtained similar results, we were shocked by the sheer magnitude of "sickness" that the therapists found in the well-functioning family.

Therapists, as our study clearly points out, are trained to find problems. They are, in other words, *problem-focused* and adept at finding "sickness"—even where none exists. This should perhaps come as no surprise since the majority of the time therapists spend in school is devoted to learning how to describe, to identify, and then to treat problems. This focus on problems and "sickness" is carried over in the publications that they read and write after becoming professional counselors. The typical alcohol counselor, for example, is bombarded with information that is, by and large, limited to the "three Ds": disease, denial, and dysfunction.

In turn, these experts churn out a plethora of books, tapes, and self-help products for public consumption that are alarmist in nature and have little or no scientific support. For example, some experts estimate that as many as 230 million adults are living with the negative effects of growing up in an alcoholic home—a figure, it turns out, that is substantially higher than the nation's total adult population.[1] Other experts have made the claim that as many as 96 percent of Americans come from dysfunctional families, despite the fact that such a figure would, by definition, make the behavior they describe normal.[2]

Unfortunately the effects of such pontificating are far from benign for the consumer of addiction and recovery literature. For example, a recent Gallup poll found that nearly 90 percent of Americans believe that science has proved that alcoholism is a disease.[3] While this may seem like a good example of modern society's ability to disseminate scientific information, the truth is that the American public has been misled. There is simply no scientific support for the notion that alcoholism is a disease. Indeed, the only scientifically verifiable result of the alcoholism-as-disease concept, as critics have pointed out, is the enrichment of the alcohol and drug treatment industry.

Some might argue that the results of our experiment exaggerate the problem of therapists focusing on the problem. Surely most therapists, they might say, are more careful when they are dealing with a living, breathing client than when they see an image of a client on a cold, technical videotape. Doesn't common sense dictate that therapists must know a lot about problems in order to be able to solve them? And what, they might ask, are we saying that therapists should focus on if they don't focus on the problem?

LISTENING TO "LITTLE GREEN MEN"

With the field's consistent focus on problems and pathology, it may not be surprising to learn that little effort has been directed toward studying the characteristics of people who manage to solve their own alcohol problems.[4] Even less effort, it so happens, has been devoted to the integration of such information into treatment. Indeed, such information has largely been considered irrelevant for understanding what causes clients to change and has even been derided in the professional discourse as "superficial." However, as the distinguished psychotherapist Paul Watzlawick has pointed out, if little green men arrived from Mars and asked counselors to explain how they had arrived at their techniques and theories for helping people change, the Martians would most likely scratch their heads in disbelief as they listened to complicated formulas about how people develop and maintain their problems, and they would probably ask why the therapists had not started their search for understanding by investigating how people change *naturally, spontaneously, and on an everyday basis.*[5] In short, the Martians might wonder why therapists had chosen to make problems rather than solutions the focus of their professional interest and activity.

Given their training, therapists, as you may have surmised, would be hard pressed to answer the Martians. However, some recent trends indicate that therapists may finally be following the advice of the little green men and becoming more solution-focused in their work. For example, just recently the field has started to study those people with alcohol problems who do not seek professional treatment but manage to overcome their problems anyway. Interestingly, despite the doom and gloom predictions of traditional treatment professionals, this research has shown that a surprisingly high number—perhaps even the majority—of people with drinking problems recover *on their own* without formal treatment.[6] By citing such research, we do not mean to imply that treatment is not necessary or that people with alcohol problems should be left to their own devices. Rather, we are saying that information about how some people spontaneously recover may be useful in helping other people with alcohol problems.

While a brief perusal of the popular recovery literature would indicate otherwise, another line of research investigating adults who grew up in alcoholic homes—so-called adult children—has actually found that a significant number—85 percent, to be exact—do not grow up to become alcoholic themselves. Rather than continue to study the 15 percent minority, psychiatrist Steven Wolin suggests that research efforts should be focused on the 85 percent majority that does not develop alcohol problems. Says Dr. Wolin: "I [believe] that this 85-percent majority who [has] resisted the noxious influence of their past [has] as much to teach us as the 15-percent minority who . . . succumb.[7]" His preliminary research has actually found evidence of some powerful common traits among people who are able to survive and even surpass their troubled upbringings. Ironically, and perhaps tragically, it is these very traits that the popular alcohol literature often labels dysfunctional, traits such as independence, initiative, empathy, tolerance for ambiguity, and humor.[8] As Wolin points out, the negative labeling of these traits may in part explain the dismal outcomes that research has documented for programs based on traditional ideas.

THE SOLUTION-FOCUSED APPROACH

Quite coincidentally the recent research closely parallels and supports our own work. Over the last twenty years we have been developing a treatment method based on the simple idea of focusing on what works. The resulting treatment method has come to be known among professional counselors and therapists as the solution-focused approach because of its distinct emphasis on solutions rather than problems. While the various techniques used in the solution-focused approach have changed and evolved over time, the basic principles have remained the same. Because the method differs so radically from popular notions about alcohol treatment, a review of these principles may help orient you to its approach.

FIRST, NO SINGLE APPROACH WORKS FOR EVERYONE.

While various experts in the field of alcohol treatment claim that "all alcoholics are ultimately alike"[9] and that people with drinking problems must adhere to the all-for-one-and-one-for-all approach of Alcoholics Anonymous if they ever hope to recover, their claims are far from the truth. Research has not shown that all alcoholics are alike. If anything, it has shown that quite the opposite is true.[10] Each person experiencing an alcohol problem is *different*. The trick of successful treatment is to design an approach that fits the unique needs of the individual client. In other words, the treatment should be tailored to fit the individual rather than require the individual to fit the treatment. Such an idea seems like common sense. However, until recently such thinking was considered heretical in the field of alcohol treatment.

In contrast with the one-size-fits-all approach of traditional alcohol treatment, solution-focused therapy, with its laserlike focus on what works, helps clients identify and then implement their own individualized plans for recovery.

SECOND, THERE ARE MANY POSSIBLE SOLUTIONS.

Just a few years ago we listened to a national expert on the treatment of alcohol problems tell a large audience of professional counselors that while "science is discovering that there are many causes for alcoholism, we all know that there is still only one solution." What is one to make of such a bold claim? Well, just imagine for a moment that you are in the market for a pair of shoes. You visit a local shoe store and find that it carries only one brand and style of shoe. Would you stay in the store? For the sake of illustration, let's say you happen to like the brand and style of shoe that the store stocks, so you choose to stay and try on a pair. When you ask the clerk to measure your foot, however, you are informed that the size of *your* foot does not matter.

The shoe, you are told, comes in only one size—the perfect size. Would you still stay in the store? Would you think about buying the shoe?

Well, if you were lucky enough to like the style of shoe the store carried and if the shoe happened to fit your foot, you might. But what would you do if the shoe did not happen to fit your foot? Would you buy the shoe then? And what would happen, as sometimes does in the field of traditional alcohol treatment, if everyone else in the store began to coax you to buy the shoe? Telling you that you are resistant, even blaming you when you try to explain to them that the shoe does not fit your foot. They press on, pointing out that since they have managed to make the shoes fit, so should you.

To those in the field who insist that one size fits all, we simply say "nonsense." Such an idea is not only wrong but downright dangerous. More people are seeking treatment for alcohol problems now than ever before. These people come from a variety of age-groups and racial and economic backgrounds. They have different histories and patterns of alcohol use. No single method of treatment could be expected to help them all. There is no solution, in other words, only *solutions*.

This is an exciting time in the field of alcohol treatment research. As old thinking gives way to new, various methods that offer more options to the person struggling with an alcohol problem are emerging and being tested. More options, of course, translate into more chances of finding something that works for you. The solution-focused approach, with its emphasis on finding a solution that works for the individual, helps clients explore a variety of possible solutions.

THIRD, THE SOLUTION AND THE PROBLEM ARE NOT NECESSARILY RELATED.

While visiting an outdoor market on a recent trip to Sweden, we noticed one vendor who was selling amulets full of powdered reindeer horn. The powder, the man explained, was a powerful aphrodisiac that was especially useful in curing male impotence. One need place only a small amount on the tongue, he assured us, in order to achieve a firm, long-lasting erection. The idea that the powderized horns of various animals are aphrodisiacs was not new to either of us. We were aware, for example, of similar notions in Chinese herbal medicine—notions which, by the way, have been responsible for the near extinction of an entire species of rhinoceros. But how, one might wonder, had these people, living in very disparate parts of the world, come up with identical ideas?

Well, before running out to buy some powdered reindeer horn, you should know that no credible scientific evidence exists for the claims that are made for these substances. To the contrary, some of these concoctions are poisonous. The idea, however, that a powdered horn could cure an erection problem stems from the overuse of a simple and often helpful idea: Causes should resemble their effects. When this idea is used appropriately, we are able to make accurate judgments and inferences. However, the inappropriate use of this idea makes us susceptible to the claims of charlatans who rely on our naïve belief that solutions (causes) should always look like the problems they are designed to solve (effects). So in the case of erection problems, since the solution should look like the problem, administering a dose of something that looks like an erection should solve the problem.

Before you go patting yourself on the back for not having fallen prey to such a silly notion, consider some other medical quackery that Americans have fallen for. Sunlight and "fertilizerlike" ointments for baldness: After all, hair looks like grass, right? Suction devices for enlarging woman's breasts: Since breasts resemble balloons, they should respond to the same laws of physics as balloons. We could go on for a long while, since the history of Western medicine also contains examples of ineffective, and in some cases dangerous, treatments that people have spent millions of dollars to acquire.

The same, unfortunately, is true of alcohol treatment. For a long time it has been assumed that the solution to alcohol problems needs to resemble the problem. Hence there has been a rapid proliferation of "specialized programs" that focus entirely on people's alcohol use. For example, we are constantly bombarded with television commercials for "recovery," "chemical dependency," and "substance abuse" programs. Thinking that the solution must look like the problem, these ads stress that help for problem drinkers can be found only in programs that focus exclusively on problem drinking. They champion abstinence as the acceptable treatment outcome and force participation in AA and other self-help groups.

However, a surprising finding from our own work is that the solution to a person's alcohol problem need not look like or even be related to that problem. Indeed, we have personally worked with and met hundreds of clients who have solved their alcohol problems by doing things that are not related to their problems in any direct fashion. These have included spending more time with the family, developing a physical exercise regimen, finding a satisfying hobby, joining a social or religious group, changing friends, eating three good meals a day, and getting a job. The list is, in fact, endless.

So that we are not misunderstood, let us state our point succinctly. The important factor is not the *particular* solution but rather any solution, however removed from the problem it may seem, that works for the individual. Einstein once said that one "cannot solve a problem with the same thinking that created it." In other words, people unfortunately limit their search for potential solutions to those that make sense in view of the problems they are trying to solve. This is certainly true, as you may have guessed, of traditional treatment. In contrast, solution-focused therapy, with its pragmatic emphasis on what works, begins by helping clients expand the range of possible solutions.

FOURTH, THE SIMPLEST AND LEAST INVASIVE APPROACH IS FREQUENTLY THE BEST MEDICINE.

Prior to the discovery of penicillin, one method that doctors used to treat the venereal disease syphilis was to infect the patient with malaria. The fever that resulted from the malaria killed the bacteria that caused the venereal disease, thereby curing the patient. The only problem with the treatment was that many of the patients died from the malaria. This is what is meant by the old saying "The treatment was successful, but the patient died!"

The history of medicine is replete with similar stories. Luckily for us, medicine has made significant strides since those early times. Moreover, with each advance there has been a concomitant decrease in the invasiveness of the treatments. For example, operations that used to take hours, require large incisions, and result in lengthy convalescence have given way to surgical procedures accomplished by lasers, inserted through small openings, and resulting in the patient's being able to return home the same day. This only stands to reason. As our knowledge about what works grows, our procedures should become simpler and less invasive.

Judging from the pessimistic pronouncements of various well-known treatment experts, one would never guess that similar advances are being made in the treatment of alcohol problems. Instead, what one hears most often is that alcohol problems seem to defy any but the most intensive and invasive of treatment procedures. For example, on the very first page of his book, one expert declares: "It is a myth that *these* people . . . seek treatment. Victims of this disease do not submit to treatment . . . they [must be] *forced* to seek help."[11] By "forcing *these* people" to see the light, this expert means removing them from their natural environments, placing them in inpatient hospital treatment programs, and forcing them to participate in highly confrontational group therapies. Never mind that Bill W., the founder of Alcoholics Anonymous, never went through an intensive inpatient alcoholism treatment program and never heard of, much less used, techniques like confrontation. The treatment is necessary, the experts argue. To do anything less, they warn, guarantees that the person will "perish miserably." Problem drinkers, the experts tell us, are never able to "stop drinking by themselves."[12]

The truth is, however, that the claims of these experts are simply not true for the majority of people with alcohol problems. As we have already mentioned, a significant number of problem drinkers and users—perhaps the majority—stop their problem use on their own. In addition, we have found, along with other researchers, that highly invasive treatment techniques like confrontation can and often do have serious consequences, not the least of which is a high dropout rate from treatment programs that employ such methods.

We realize that this information may not be new to you. Indeed, you, or someone you love, may already have experienced failure in traditional treatment. Whatever you do, however, don't give in to the temptation to blame yourself or your loved one. Traditional treatment professionals delight in explaining away treatment failures by "blaming the patient." For example, you, or someone you love, may have been told that the failure to respond to the treatment was due to "denial" or "resistance." You may even have been told that your family history is too dysfunctional to respond to one treatment or that you "haven't hit bottom yet."

To this, and all other attempts to blame treatment failures solely on the client, we simply say "nonsense." More than likely, the truth is that you have just not found something that works for you yet. Don't give up. While these programs tout various "success rates" as evidence of their efficacy, research has consistently found that the relapse rates for the traditional treatment programs hover around 90 percent! And most of these relapses occur very shortly after clients have been discharged from the various programs. Other studies have shown that the components of these programs simply teach people to return for more treatment, not to solve their drinking problems. This occurs so frequently that treatment professionals have even given it a name: the revolving door phenomenon.

The high dropout and relapse rates of traditional programs have led us to conclude that complex and invasive procedures like inpatient treatment and confrontation are not the treatments of choice for most people with alcohol problems. As Kendrick, one of our former clients, once said of his three hospitalizations, "You sit up there with thirty to forty people and everybody has got the same problem you've got. You learn all about the phases of drug and alcohol addiction, you talk about your habit and what you have done with drugs, you talk about your family and their drinking and what you went through as a child, but nobody has any answers—none that worked for me anyway."

After being labeled "difficult" by treatment professionals during his third try in the traditional program, Kendrick was discharged early and told to come back when he was "serious about doing something to change his drug and alcohol problem." Luckily he did not give up. Once in treatment with us, Kendrick was able to develop a personalized program of recovery that worked for him in the "real world." Professionals and clients working together to develop a simple, straightforward, flexible, and individualized program of recovery are one of the hallmarks of the solution-focused approach. Indeed, someone once said that we "settle for any dirty little solution that works." We take that as a compliment.

FIFTH, PEOPLE CAN AND DO GET BETTER QUICKLY.

Although the traditional assumption that alcoholism is a disease logically results in the conclusion that recovery will be a long-term process, our research and our clinical experience suggest that clients want to and do recover from alcohol problems rather rapidly. While each client is different, the majority of those treated with this method are seen for only a handful of sessions.[13] Long-term treatment is clearly the exception to the rule and, more often than not, has little or no correlation with the severity or chronicity of the person's drinking problem.[14] Similar findings led researchers at the prestigious Institute of Medicine in Washington, D.C., to conclude that there should be a significant shift of resources away from long-term, recovery-oriented approaches and toward more efficient and individualized treatment approaches.[15]

To say that success can be accomplished rapidly is, however, not the same as saying that it is easy. Indeed, we often warn our clients that solving their problem will require hard work on their part—perhaps the hardest work they have ever done in their lives. We have found that our clients are rarely surprised by our warning. *They* know that dealing with their alcohol problem is not a simple matter of "Just say no!" Being warned, they set more realistic expectations and are prepared when faced by the challenges that inevitably accompany recovery.

How, you might reasonably ask, is it possible to say in the same breath both that recovery is hard work and that it can be accomplished rapidly? The answer lies in the next principle of solution-focused work.

SIXTH, CHANGE IS HAPPENING ALL THE TIME.

Stability is an illusion. To illustrate this point, we often tell our trainees and clients that life is a lot more like a river than a lake. Far from being static, in other words, people are in a constant state of flux as they change and adapt to the course of life. Very often, successful treatment turns on identifying these naturally occurring changes and helping people use them deliberately to bring about solutions. We have found, in other words, that success results from learning to go with the flow of the river rather than from damming it up.

While the idea that change is inevitable is not a new one in the history of humankind, it is an unusual notion in the field of mental health. Traditional treatment assumes that change is not only *not* inevitable but in most cases unlikely. Traditional theories and methods assume that problems are constant in nature. One expression typical of this type of pessimistic attitude is heard at least once in nearly all traditional programs: "Once an alcoholic always an alcoholic." In most cases the only inevitable change ever acknowledged by traditional programs is one for the worse. Consider once again the viewpoint of Vernon Johnson, one of the leading experts in traditional alcohol treatment: "Unless the chemically dependent person gets help, he or she will die . . . chemical dependency is progressive . . . [and] this means that it always gets worse."[16]

Experts aside, our experience with our problem drinking clients is that change for the better is at least as likely to occur as change for the worse, if not more so. Nothing happens all the time. There is, in another words, always an exception, so that identifying and building on previous successes and ongoing change are key ingredients of solution-focused work. Take, for example, the case of Roger, a fifty-four-year-old self-described "alcoholic" man who came to us for help after a two-month-long binge that had nearly cost him his life. Roger said that he had been drinking constantly since he was "very young" and had been in a number of different treatment programs over the years. When we asked him if there had ever been periods of time during which he had successfully managed his problems with alcohol, he looked at us and, somewhat puzzled, responded that there had indeed been times when alcohol was not a problem for him. Not only had he somehow managed to stop drinking prior to seeing us, but he was also able to identify long periods—months and years, in fact—during which he had successfully managed to curb his drinking. Pushed for details, Roger was able to specify exactly what he had done during those periods that contributed to his success. In the end the only thing we did was help Roger develop a plan for doing the things that had worked before.[17]

SEVENTH, FOCUS ON STRENGTHS AND RESOURCES RATHER THAN WEAKNESSES AND DEFICITS.

Not long ago we were conducting a two-day workshop on solution-focused therapy. As sometimes happens, one therapist in the audience spent the majority of the first day raising objections and making angry comments to those seated around her about the material we were presenting. "We were," she informed us and the members of the audience, "clearly in denial!"

To our surprise, the woman returned the next day and sat quietly, taking notes throughout the workshop. Surprise quickly gave way to paranoia, however, when she approached us at the conclusion of the workshop and asked to meet us privately. Not long before, colleagues of ours had been pelted with eggs and received death threats after challenging some of the cherished claims of the traditional approach.

The woman started the private meeting by telling us how angry she had been the preceding day. These feelings, she informed us, stayed with her long after leaving the workshop. Disturbed by their intensity, the woman spent most of the evening trying to figure out why she was so upset. After much thinking, she told us, she finally realized the source of her anger. The woman, a therapist herself, had been in therapy for the nearly ten years. "Not once in all that time," the woman now said through her tears, "has my therapist told me anything that is right in my life!" .

The therapist's story is not only sad but tragically common. People's strengths and resources have traditionally been ignored because of the commonsense notion that problems result from some underlying weakness or deficit. These deficits, we are told by the experts, must be addressed if we ever hope to solve our problems. To this effect, therapists have offered a never-ending list of weaknesses: permissive parenting and strict parenting, restrictive toilet training and indulgent toilet training, lack of breast feeding and too much breast feeding, etc. Most recently the experts have touted the "wounded inner child" as the cause of all our misery. The contradictory, inconsistent quality of their advice, however, can lead one to wonder if the experts know what they are talking about.[18]

One thing they seem to know for certain, however, is that you are sick. Your only hope is to uncover and accept your weaknesses and deficits. Indeed, the very first step of Alcoholics Anonymous is to admit that one is powerless over alcohol. To this and all other prophecies of doom, we once again say "nonsense!" People are not powerless over alcohol, and they never were. There is simply no research to support the idea that people cannot control their drinking; in fact, as with almost everything else the popular recovery movement espouses, the research indicates that the opposite may be true. People are able to take charge of and manage their problem drinking. What seems to matter is whether or not the person *believes* he or she can control his or her drinking. This was demonstrated very clearly in a classic study on the effects of alcohol.

Researchers divided alcoholics into four groups. Members of each group were asked to rate the taste of three different beverages and told that they could consume as much of the beverage as they wanted.[19] The four groups differed only in what they were led to believe about the beverages. Members of one group were told that they were being offered three different types of drinks containing alcohol when they were, in fact, being offered nonalcoholic beverages. The second group was led to believe that the three drinks contained no alcohol when in fact, all three contained alcohol. The third group was given nonalcoholic drinks and told they contained no alcohol, while the last group was given alcoholic beverages and told they contained alcohol. Each group was then given time to taste-test the three beverages. Interestingly, for the two groups that were misled, the researchers found that the amount that people drank was related to how much alcohol they *thought* was in the drink, not the actual amount in the drink.

The research confirms what the famous psychologist William

James observed nearly a hundred years ago: "The greatest discovery of my generation is that human beings, by changing the
inner attitudes of their minds, can change the outer aspects of
their lives. It is too bad that more people will not accept this
tremendous discovery and begin living it."[20]

Like James and these researchers, we have found that what
people believe about themselves and alcohol can have a profound impact on the outcome of treatment. People with alcohol
problems are *not* inherently powerless over these substances.
Indeed, the people whom we have worked with display a variety
of skills and resources that they can bring to bear on their alcohol problems. These strengths are a better guide to recovery
than are their weaknesses. Uncovering strengths and integrating
them into a personalized recovery program are a strategy that
consistently works for people with alcohol problems.

It is not uncommon for a people's strengths to be buried
under a mountain of guilt and shame about their childhood, personal failures, or alcohol problems. Moreover, the fact that people's strengths are not always immediately obvious may be the
reason why the entire popular recovery movement has been
misled into believing that they do not exist. Nothing, however,
could be further from the truth. For example, Dr. Wolin's recent research has found that while the traditional assumption for
years has been that "misfortune during childhood necessarily
leads to decreased psychological functioning in adults . . . we are
seeing that children can cope with adversity and that, ironically,
an increased sense of personal competence can result from successfully meeting the challenges of a troubled family."[21] So
whether you grew up in an alcoholic home, suffered abuse at the
hand of a loved one, or developed a problem with alcohol later
in life, you still have strengths and resources that can be used to
deal with your current problem.

Let us state our point clearly. Saying that a person has
strengths and resources does not mean that people do not have
pain or that their pain is unimportant. Quite the contrary, if peo-

ple weren't in pain, they would probably not go for help or read self-help books such as this one. Pain is a great motivator. However, saying that pain motivates us to seek help is not the same as saying that it holds the solution. For some reason, focusing on pain, weakness, and deficits has become standard operating procedure in treatment. Everywhere people are seeing therapists and gathering in self-help groups and being led to talk about their pain. Indeed, pushing people to confess their pain and weakness has become so much a part of the popular culture surrounding therapy that one psychoanalyst has said that most therapy can be described as "two people sitting alone in a room talking until one of them cries."[22] Pain may get us started, but strengths and resources help us stay on track and finish the job.

EIGHTH, FOCUS ON THE FUTURE RATHER THAN THE PAST.

Traditional treatment approaches have been on an psychoarchaeology expedition almost from their inception. That is, romance with the past, combined with a belief in the age-old admonition that the "sins of the fathers shall be visited upon the sons," has led practitioners to believe that the road to recovery begins by unlocking the gate of the past. Hundreds and perhaps thousands of people have been encouraged to search for solutions to their current problems by inspecting their childhoods for damage. It could be argued that convincing people that their problems are caused by childhood events was one of the great marketing successes of the twentieth century. The whole idea that problems are rooted in childhood has now become a popular part of American culture. Even a brief sampling of today's television talk shows and print media shows how discussion of the past has slipped out of the therapist's office into the everyday life of Americans.

So zany has this trek into the past become that some mental health professionals are insisting that problems result not so much from our earlier as from our past lives! In the spirit of traditional treatment, these professionals advocate focusing on the past; this time, however, looking for solutions in the past is accomplished by using hypnosis to regress people to their *previous* lives. Despite an absolute lack of scientific, psychological, and medical evidence to support such treatments, the practice is actually growing in popularity. One can only speculate about how such beliefs will play out in American culture in the future.[23]

We believe that it is not necessary to know where you have come from in order to figure out where you would like to go. Quite the contrary. All that is necessary is some type of road map that shows you where you want to get to from where you are right now. Therapy is increasingly viewed as the solution to a host of problems that plague our society. However, as one well-known therapist has observed, "Therapy is not the solution, it is the problem. The solution is getting people out of therapy!"[24]

Successful treatment of alcohol problems begins by figuring out how the treatment will end. "If you don't know where you are going, you will probably end up someplace else," an old saying goes. Rather than go on a "bone hunt," solution-focused work begins by helping people develop concrete, realistic maps of where they would like to go. This is why we constantly ask our clients how they will know when they are done with treatment—how they will know, in other words, when we can stop meeting like this.

These are the basic principles of solution-focused work. Before we go any further, however, we want to make it clear that no one book—and no one treatment method, for that matter—can help everyone. When we gave up working in traditional ways, we also abandoned any hope we might have had of discovering the right way to help people recover from alcohol problems. The complex nature of the problem defies a simple uniform "one-size-fits-all" solution. In the continuing battle against alcohol problems, what is needed is not *the* answer but many answers, not one possible treatment but many treatment possibilities, not believers in the true way but a way for people to find a truth they can believe in. What is needed, in other words, is a focus on what works.

THE READY REFERENCE

Our focus on what works has led us to create what we call "The Miracle Method Ready Reference" system. At the conclusion of each chapter you will find a summary of the important points of that chapter. We have created this system because we found that being mindful of the various ideas, strategies, and techniques was often half of the battle for our problem drinking clients. If they somehow managed to keep the ideas in their minds, they dramatically increased the chances that their behavior would be affected for the better.

Since keeping the principles of the solution-focused approach in mind is one of the things we have found that "works" with problem drinkers, we end this chapter with the first of these ready references.

THE MIRACLE METHOD
READY REFERENCE

❑

PRINCIPLES OF THE
SOLUTION-FOCUSED APPROACH

1. No single approach works for everyone.
2. There are many possible solutions.
3. The solution and the problem are not necessarily related.
4. The simplest and least invasive approach is frequently the best medicine.
5. People can and do get better quickly.
6. Change is happening all the time.
7. Focus on strengths and resources rather than weaknesses and deficits.
8. Focus on the future rather than the past.

3

Unlocking the Door
to Solution

SIX KEYS FOR SUCCESS

> In dreams we do so many things,
> we set aside the rules we know.
> And fly above the world so high
> in great and shining rings.
> If only we could always live in dreams,
> *if only we could make of life what in dreams*
> *it seems. . . .*
> —W. Jennings and R. Kerr, "In the Real World"

> Some people see problems and ask why. I dream
> dreams and ask why not.
> —Robert F. Kennedy

> Where there is no vision, the people perish.
> —Proverbs 29:18

In one of our favorite episodes of "M*A*S*H," Corporal Klinger, who is usually caught feigning some type of medical or psychological malady in order to escape the service, really becomes ill. At the beginning of the episode, Captains Hunnicut and Pierce are hard at work to find the correct diagnosis for the illness that has caused Klinger to develop a high fever and become delirious. Worried that the high fever may kill Klinger if it is not diagnosed and treated properly, Pierce and Hunnicut explore a series of possible causes. As they argue over the correct diagnosis of the mystery illness, however, Klinger's condition worsens, and he begins hallucinating a conversation with a dead soldier. Their disagreement eventually brings Nurse Houlihan and Colonel Potter into the discussion. Together Hunnicut, Pierce, Houlihan, and Potter discuss, explore, and argue about the illness affecting Klinger, who by this time is lapsing into a coma.

At some point near the end of the show all agree that finding out the correct diagnosis will have to take a backseat to bringing Klinger's high temperature under control. Otherwise Klinger may die! With little discussion they all rapidly agree to pack the corporal in ice. Klinger's temperature, of course, immediately begins to drop and the life-and-death crisis passes. Colonel Potter, reflecting on the difficulty he and his fellow officers had in solving the problem, observes, "We were so busy trying to figure out what the problem was that we ignored *the obvious solution!*"

THE OBVIOUS SOLUTION

Right now in the field of alcohol treatment Corporal Klinger is dying while thousands of professionals are arguing about what is killing him. That is, they are spending a lot of time helping people unravel the supposedly correct, clear causes of the problems that trouble them. Indeed, the field has no shortage of potential explanations for problems resulting from alcohol use. We hear, for example, of "dysfunctional families," "codependency," and the "adult child of alcoholic syndrome," the "alcoholic personality," and the "genetic basis for alcoholism."

Not only is there little scientific support for such ideas, but they simply do not tell us the best way to go about solving the problem. Moreover, when one assumes that the solution is determined by the problem, some strange and even unhelpful practices are likely to emerge. For example, one frequently hears experts saying that most mental health problems—problem drinking included—stem from emotions that have been repressed. In the jargon of pop psychology, these emotions are said to have been "stuffed." Where these emotions are "stuffed" is not entirely clear, but what one is supposed to do about them, according to the experts, is: express them, talk about them, "get them out!" In books, in articles, and on popular television talk shows, "stuffed" feelings are touted as the cause of many of the problems facing people in our society.

This is particularly true of the advice experts give about anger. Anger, we are told, has reached epidemic proportions in our society. How do we know? One prime example is the increasing amount of violence in our society. Violence, the experts say, is due to a general inability to express angry feelings. Not expressing the anger, they warn, results in the dire consequences one sees on the television news every evening! When we reason from the supposed cause, we find, of course, that the cure is to express the anger. To judge from the increasing amount of violence in our society, however, it seems to us that the problem is that people are not stuffing their anger enough. Indeed, one could justifiably argue that the increase in violence comes not from people's "stuffing" their angry feelings but precisely from their following the ever-present counsel to "let it all hang out."

So what is the obvious solution? You already know a lot about your problem. And you probably would not be reading this book if you did not want to do something about it. Like Corporal Klinger, what you don't need is a group of experts sitting around trying to help you figure out what your diagnosis is (i.e., problem drinker, alcoholic, or alcoholic personality) or what is causing the alcohol problem that is troubling you (e.g., dysfunctional family history, adult child of alcoholic syndrome, codependency, or genetics). Indeed, we often find that *people resort to explanations of their behavior when they have not been able to change it.* This tendency is true for experts as well.

When Colonel Potter, Nurse Houlihan, and Captains Hunnicut and Pierce finally give up looking for the cause of Klinger's ailment and focus instead on the problem they want to solve, the obvious solution emerges very quickly. How do they do this? They focus on what they want to be different—in this case, for Klinger's temperature to come down. In other words, they focus on the outcome, the goal, or the solution that they want rather than on the diagnosis, problem, or difficulty that they do not want.

The obvious solution to problem drinking is to figure out exactly what you want to be different when the problem that is troubling you is solved. The more clearly you are able to specify exactly how you want things to be different after your problem is solved, the more likely it is that you will be able to unlock the door to that solution. In this chapter we will describe six specific "keys" for unlocking that door. First, however, let's get you to the door.

THE DOOR TO SOLUTION

Recently a prominent researcher in the field of alcohol treatment conducted an interesting study.[1] The researcher divided people with drinking problems into two groups. Each group was then exposed to one of four different types of treatment. These treatments ranged from least intensive on the one end to most intensive on the other end. The only real difference between the two groups was that the people in the first group were allowed to choose which of the four treatments they wanted, whereas the people in the second group were *assigned* to one of the four treatments.

The most important result of this study was that the people who were given a choice were much more likely to work hard to solve their problem than those who were not. A second result of the study was that the people who were given a choice were more likely to ask for additional help if it was needed than those who were not. As a matter of fact, those people who were forced into a treatment that they did not choose were less likely to solve their problem, more likely to drop out of treatment, and less likely to seek additional help even though they might need some.

The results of this study confirm the commonsense notion that "You can lead a horse to water, but you can't make it drink." The same results, however, contradict the philosophy of most traditional treatment programs which holds that people with alcohol problems are uniformly "out of touch with reality" and must be forced into treatment. As the research suggests, however, heavy confrontation and lack of choice about treatment options combine to cause the poor treatment outcomes often found in programs that espouse such heavy-handed tactics.[2] The implications of the research are that people should not be forced through a particular door but encouraged to find a door that they are interested and invested in opening. Finding the door to solution then begins with the choice "I want my life to be different in some way, my way." The problem drinker should not be "pushed or prodded," the *Big Book* advises, "the desire must come from within."[3]

> Finding the "door to solution"
> begins with *choice*.

How, you might reasonably ask, can you go about finding the right door to choose? Back in 1984 one of our clients showed us the way. A woman called us for an appointment, demanding that she be seen that day because it was an emergency. She began sobbing as she told the receptionist how her husband's drinking was out of control and that he had even been violent toward her. Mary, as we shall call her, was still tearful when she arrived for her scheduled appointment later that day. As she entered the therapist's office and began to sit down, she said, "My problem is so serious that it will take a *miracle* to solve it!" Following her lead, the therapist simply said, "Well, Mary, suppose one happened. . . ?"

After a few moments of silent thought Mary began to describe what she wanted to be different about the situation that was troubling her. As she described what she wanted in more detail, a smile began to creep into her face and the tone of her voice became more hopeful. By the end of the session Mary had described precisely the direction that she wanted to go. As she stood to leave the office, she told the therapist that she was feeling "much better." The following week Mary returned and reported that she had turned that feeling into some small but significant changes in her life and her marriage.

The success that we experienced with Mary led us to begin asking all our clients to pretend during the session that a miracle had solved their problem. Surprisingly we found that other clients responded like Mary. For example, we observed that clients experiencing a wide variety of personal and family problems, ranging from mild to very serious, became more hopeful and returned with reports of having taken steps in the desired direction. Indeed, many people found that they were already experiencing some of what they wanted once they were able to state it clearly by thinking about the miracle's happening.

Over the years we have found that asking clients this miracle question helps people find their own doors to solution. You can find your door to solution by taking the time to ask this question of yourself now.

> The door to solution is opened by considering how you want your life to be different once your problem has been solved.

Don't be discouraged and give up if you have some difficulty when you first try to imagine how your situation would be different if a miracle happened. Be patient with yourself. As we pointed out in the last chapter, we usually don't think about the solution that we want; we usually think about the problem that we have. Here goes:

> Suppose tonight, after you go to bed and fall asleep, while you are sleeping, a miracle happens. The miracle is that the problem or problems you are struggling with are solved! Just like that! Since you are sleeping, however, you don't know that the miracle has happened. You sleep right through the whole event. When you wake up tomorrow morning, *what would be some of the first things* that you would notice that would be different and that would tell you that the miracle has happened and that your problem is solved?

Take some time right now to consider your answer carefully. Most people find it helpful to commit their answers to paper. If you haven't already done so, now would be a good time to start that notebook we mentioned in the first chapter. Your first entry can be your answer to the miracle question.

If you are the type of person who learns best by watching or listening to others, you may find it useful to read the answer that one of our clients gave to the miracle question before you try the question yourself. We will use dialogue from this actual case with a problem drinker throughout this chapter to illustrate the miracle question as well as other important points.

❏

DRINKING ON THE DOCKS

Lee was a thirty-six-year-old foreman for a large trucking company. He had been promoted to the job of foreman after a relatively short time as a dock worker as the result of his willingness to work hard and of what his employers called his can-do attitude. Lee had taken great pride in receiving the promotion. No one in the company's history had been promoted so rapidly.

Lee's rapid rise in the company came with a stiff price, however. Being foreman had, for example, dramatically increased his workload and responsibilities. Even more troublesome, however, were the changes between Lee and his former co-workers and friends on the loading dock. Many, jealous of his success, now refused to speak to him. Some even did things to sabotage work on the loading dock. At first Lee had applied the same can-do attitude to the changes in his relationships and the problems on the loading platform. Eventually, however, he began to drink as a way of coping with the new stresses and loneliness.

By the time Lee came to see us, his job as foreman was in jeopardy. His performance had deteriorated over the last few months, and management had recently discovered that he was drinking on the job. After Lee had a chance to tell us his story, we asked him the "miracle" question.[4]

THERAPIST: Lee, let me ask you a strange kind of question.
LEE: Okay.
TH: It takes some pretending on your part.
LEE: Yeah, shoot.
TH: Okay. Suppose tonight, after our meeting, you go home, go to bed, and fall asleep.
LEE: I'm with you so far.
TH: And while you are sleeping, *a miracle happens.*
LEE: Uh-huh.
TH: The miracle is that the problem or problems you are struggling with are solved!
LEE: I no longer have these problems.
TH: Yes. Just like that! Your problems are solved. Since you are sleeping, however, you don't know that the miracle has happened. You sleep right through the whole event.

When you wake up tomorrow morning, what would be some of the first things that you would notice that would be different and that would tell you that a miracle has happened and that your problem is solved?

LEE *(pause):* I wouldn't feel like I am having to exert all of my energy to keep things in check.

TH: Uh-huh.

LEE: I would be living my life again. I wouldn't be so gloomy and negative. I would be more happy and positive. I would be smiling at work and maybe even laughing.

TH: Uh-huh. What else?

LEE: I wouldn't have this wrinkled brow and knotted-up forehead all the time, and I wouldn't have this ache in my chest. I would get out and move around again. Right now all I do is just stay at my desk. So I would go out and talk to the guys on the dock. No matter what they did. Nowadays I just hide, you see.

TH: Uh-huh.

LEE *(with surprise):* Oh, I know. I wouldn't come home from work and solve all my problems by drinking. Maybe I wouldn't stop by the bar and complain to Ted [the bartender] about the guys on the dock. "Oh, you shoulda seen those SOBs today," you know. My whole conversation wouldn't be negative.

TH: Anything else that would be different after the miracle?

LEE *(long pause):* Maybe work wouldn't be my entire life. Maybe, like I said, I would start living my life again. You know, I got this great job, and I haven't done anything for myself since.

☐

Lee's answer continued for a while longer. As he continued to speak, he began to smile and his mood brightened considerably.

BE PATIENT WITH YOURSELF

Not all clients are able to answer the miracle question as quickly as Lee. Sometimes they have to think about the miracle for a few hours (or even days) before an answer begins to take shape. When you have been thinking in a certain way about your problem, it can take awhile to shift to a new perspective. After some time, however, you will start to envision an alternate reality, a reality that contains the solution rather than the problem. As was the case with Lee, more than one reality may occur to you. That's fine. Don't limit yourself at this early stage in the process. Now is the time to consider all possible avenues of success. The more possible avenues, the more chances there are for approaching your door to solution. Just let your mind wander. Be like one of our clients who described the experience of answering the miracle question as "running down a hallway of doors and opening each one along the way." At present you don't have to decide which door to choose. You simply need to know what the choices are.

As happened with Lee, being able to visualize the solution or solutions will result in your feeling a renewed sense of hope and encouragement about the possibility of solving the problem that you have. And feeling hope and encouragement is often the first step in taking the actions necessary to change your life. By the way, *don't be surprised if your answer to the question has nothing to do with the problem you are struggling with.* After all, the question assumes that the problem is solved!

THE SIX KEYS

Once you have arrived at your door to solution, you will need the right key or combination of keys in order to open it. Over the years we have found several keys that seem to work for many doors. As you read about these keys, you will be challenged to refine your answer to the miracle question in a way that will increase the likelihood that your desired solution will occur. Consider each key carefully and in detail, since you can never know in advance which one will open your door to solution.

KEY 1: MAKE SURE YOUR MIRACLE IS IMPORTANT TO YOU.

People are more likely to work hard to achieve a solution when it is one that is important to them. Indeed, we have found that there is an inverse relationship between people's level of motivation and whether they are working to achieve something that they really don't care about. The research study that we reviewed on page 35 showed this as well.

For years, however, traditional treatment approaches have made it a practice to talk problem drinkers into solutions in which they have little interest or investment. Confrontation, family intervention, and inpatient programs in hospitals have been used to "force" clients to "see the light" and accept such solutions. The high rates of relapse from such programs should come as no surprise since the participants are not working on their own solutions.

Our own experience and the latest research confirm our long-held belief that people know what they want and are most successful when they are encouraged to develop their own solutions. Professionals in the field of alcohol treatment, ourselves included, are continually learning. For most of the history of the field, professionals have assumed that they know what is best for people with alcohol problems. Of course, the research has proved otherwise. Indeed, reviewing the research on the success rates of alcohol treatment approaches is humbling, if not humiliating.

Take, for example, a study conducted in England.[5] Researchers there divided a group of severe problem drinkers into two groups. Those in the first group received only one session of therapy with a psychiatrist who told them that they were suffering from alcoholism and recommended that they abstain from all drink. The second group was offered an intensive yearlong program that included personal counseling, participation in AA, and drugs to relieve withdrawal symptoms and make alcohol consumption unpalatable. These problem drinkers were also offered admission to an inpatient hospital treatment program if they so desired. After a year the problem drinkers from the two groups were evaluated. Contrary to what one might expect, those in the second group were no better off than those in the first group, the ones who received only a single session of advice.

Therefore, telling you what to do to solve your problem will not work. The most useful approach is to help you figure out what is important to you and how you can obtain it. For this reason, make sure your answer to the miracle question is something that is personally beneficial to *you,* something that *you* want to be different, something that will make a difference in *your* life once it happens. Don't let others tell you what you should want to work on. Work on what you want to work on. Here are some questions that you can ask yourself to make sure that your answer to the miracle question is important to you:

- If the miracle happened, would that make a difference for you?
- What will you notice different about yourself when the miracle happens?
- What will others (spouse, friends, children, employer) notice different about you when the miracle happens?
- What difference will it make in your life when the miracle happens?
- What will you be able to do after the miracle happens that you could not do before?

Some examples of solutions that were important to the problem drinkers whom we have worked with have been getting someone (such as parent, employer, or spouse) "off their backs," complying with the conditions of probation or parole, improving a relationship or marriage, developing new friendships, exploring a new hobby, and so on.

Recall the case of the foreman Lee? His answers to the miracle question were clearly about what was important to him. He spoke of having a better attitude, being happier and more positive, interacting with the employees he supervised regardless of their attitude or behavior toward him, not solving his problems with alcohol, and regaining a life outside work. We knew these answers were important to Lee because of the impact they had on his mood and behavior during the session. Remember that he began to smile and feel more encouraged as he discussed the outcome he desired.

KEY 2: KEEP IT SMALL.

Contrary to traditional belief, we find that the majority of people suffering from alcohol problems want to succeed. Rather than being "in denial" or "resistant," these people are all too willing to set extraordinarily high standards for themselves. When they fail to live up to these standards, however, they feel as if they have failed, and they become discouraged about their prospects for success.

Those close to problem drinkers quite understandably become discouraged as well. Problem drinkers often make large promises to these important others in a genuine effort to please them. This happens in relationships with professionals as well. Confusing determination with ability, the traditional counselor unwittingly allows the problem drinker to set up unreasonably high expectations for success. A sampling of such expectations includes: promising never to use alcohol again, attending ninety meetings in ninety days, completely abstaining from all alcohol, etc. When clients fail to live up to these impossibly high standards, professional counselors may blame them by saying that they lack determination, don't want to change, have not dedicated themselves to the recovery process, or are fooling themselves. They may even say that failure is an inevitable part of that process!

As may already be obvious, however, the problem is usually not a lack of determination but a failure to develop reasonable expectations of success. If your goals are too big, you will fail more than you succeed. The problem with this is that it is difficult to maintain the determination you need to solve your problem when everything you try ends in failure. In this regard, we always counsel our problem drinking clients to think small. Strangely enough, this is what is advocated in the AA slogan "Keep it simple, stupid!"

When we first ask our clients the miracle question, it is not uncommon to hear statements like "I shall never drink again," "My whole life will be together," or "I shall go to ninety meetings in ninety days." These expectations are too big and almost guaranteed to result in failure. We are not asking you to think about how your life would be if you were perfect. Rather, the miracle question asks you specifically to consider the *first signs* of change you notice. Rather than "never drinking again," more reasonable expectations might be eating healthy meals, cutting down from five drinks to two, going for walks, calling a friend, getting out of the house, holding hands with your spouse, driving a different way home that does not pass the bar, and getting up on time for work in the morning.

□

SOUNDING THE ALARM FOR CHANGE: MILLIE'S STORY

Not long ago a woman in her fifties whom we shall call Millie came for the treatment of a serious alcohol problem. She told us that she had been drinking heavily for nearly twenty-five years and had been through a number of traditional inpatient and outpatient treatment programs. Millie had learned all the slogans and buzzwords of AA during her many previous treatments, and she used them to describe herself and her drinking problem to us. Despite having been through the programs and learning all the special phrases and words, Millie still had a serious drinking problem. Now her health was failing and her husband was threatening to leave their thirty-year marriage.

After posing the miracle question, we asked Millie what the first small sign of success would be. She told us that it would be that she got out of bed by eight o'clock in the morning rather than slept until noon. When we asked her if she had ever done this before, she paused to think and then began smiling widely as she reported that she had, in fact, arisen earlier in the morning not long ago. With great surprise, Millie then remembered that she had not drunk that day.

❏

Here are some questions you can ask yourself to help in this process:

- What would be the very first sign that the miracle had happened?
- What would be the smallest thing that could be different and you would still notice?
- What would be the smallest change you would settle for?
- On a scale from 1 to 10, in which 1 is where you are right now and 10 is the day after the miracle, what will be different when you move up the scale to 1.25? To 1.5? To 2?

As was the case with Millie, you can check whether or not your expectations are small enough by asking yourself if any of the small changes that you have identified have ever happened before. If your answer is no, then it is likely that you are setting your expectations too high.

KEY 3: MAKE IT SPECIFIC, CONCRETE, AND BEHAVIORAL.

In the popular recovery movement one often hears talk of the supposed diseases that trouble problem drinkers and their loved ones. Problem drinkers, for example, are said to have the incurable disease of addiction, their loved ones are said to be coalcoholics or codependents, and the children of problem drinkers are now labeled as having their own syndrome. All are said to suffer from a lack of "self-esteem" and to be in dire need of treatment to help them take control of their respective diseases, build appropriate relationship boundaries, and deal with the aftereffects of alcohol in their lives. The experts warn consumers, however, that treatment must not be thought of as a discrete event but, according to popular recovery guru Vernon E. Johnson, as a "process and life-long commitment."[6]

When one considers how vague these "diseases" are, it is not difficult to figure out why the experts say it will take a lifetime to deal successfully with them. The difficulty with using vague diseases as a guide for dealing with alcohol problems is precisely that they make it nearly impossible to figure out whether or not progress is being made. For example, how can one possibly know when he or she has licked the disease? Is no longer codependent? Has dealt with issues stemming from being an "adult child"? A person could conceivably work on these issues for a lifetime. This is not because they require a lifetime to solve, however, but because they are so vague that it is not possible to know when one is finished! What's more, who can ever have too much of some of these things—for example, self-esteem? Is there a point at which someone can have too much self-esteem?

Another, perhaps larger problem with using such vague problems as guides to treatment is that they may actually prevent people who are experiencing success with their alcohol problems from moving on to other important issues that require their attention—for example, family or marriage problems. This only stands to reason. If you cannot be sure that you are making progress on something you are working hard on, you are likely to stay in one place, repeating the same strategies or solving that problem again and again. Or if you are like some problem drinkers, you may give up and quit trying altogether.

Over the years we have met with a number of former problem drinkers who express confusion about why they no longer have drinking problems even though they have not attended recovery-oriented programs for years. Many have actually told us that they have returned to normal drinking in their lives. Are they doing something wrong? they ask us. The confusion is understandable because of what the popular recovery movement teaches and because of the incessant predictions of dire consequences if problem drinkers do not remain ever vigilant and committed to lifelong recovery. Our answer is, of course, no, they are actually doing something right. In contrast with traditional treatment, in solution-focused therapy we spend the majority of time helping people to understand specifically what they have done in order to be successful and then to move on with their lives. These are or should be the goals for any treatment: *solving your problem and getting you back to the business of living your life as quickly as possible.* "Therapy is not the solution," the well-known therapist Jay Haley once said; "it is the problem! The solution is to get clients out of therapy."[7] The bottom line is that you shouldn't have to spend your entire life in treatment or aftercare programs in order to resolve your drinking problem. Believe it or not, this is a new idea and experience for many therapists. Indeed, one therapist, surprised by his success in treating clients with this method, said, "After becoming solution-focused in my work, I have actually been able to finish treatment with some of my clients!"[8]

Therefore, as you go about describing how things will be different after the miracle, be sure that your descriptions are in concrete, specific, and behavioral terms. You need to know when you are finished, when you have been successful. In evaluating whether your stated objectives are specific enough, ask yourself the following questions:

1. When the miracle happens, will I be able to count it?
2. When the miracle is happening, will I be able to point at it?
3. Could I take a picture of the miracle as it is unfolding?

If your answers are an unqualified yes, you are probably on the right track. Such descriptions will allow you to know both when you are making progress and, once progress has been made, what else remains to be accomplished. If you answer no to any of the questions, go back and try to make your description more specific. Here is one helpful hint: Stay away from the popular psychological jargon—what we call therapy-speak—that characterizes most self-help books and the popular recovery movement. This includes such psychobabble as "developing appropriate boundaries," "learning to communicate," "improving your self-esteem," "dealing with your adult child issues," "overcoming your codependency," or "getting in touch with your inner child." Having any of these as your door to solution is guaranteed to keep that door locked up tight.

In order to help you further describe your miracle in specific, concrete, and behavioral terms, take time to answer the following questions:

• What will you notice yourself doing differently the day after the miracle that will tell you that you are on track?
• What will others see you doing that will tell them a miracle has happened? What exactly will they see that will tell them?
• Suppose we were watching you on television the day after the miracle. What would we see that would tell us the miracle has taken place?

If you are still struggling to become more specific, consider answering these questions:

• How will you know when you are (communicating, have more self-esteem, are dealing with your codependency, etc.)?

- What will you notice that is different when you have (dealt successfully with your codependency, problem drinking, etc.)?
- When you say (insert vague statement here), what exactly do you mean, and what will you be doing that is different when you no longer have this problem? What will others notice that is different when you no longer have this problem?

❑

BACK TO THE LOADING DOCK

Let's return for a moment to the case of Lee, the foreman on the loading dock whom you read about earlier, and illustrate this important key with dialogue from his session with the therapist. You will recall that Lee gave a few specific, concrete, and behavioral answers in his response to the miracle question. For example, he mentioned he would be "smiling at work" and talking once again "to the guys on the dock." You will also recall, however, that Lee said he would be "happy and positive" and doing more things for himself. While these answers may seem specific—after all, everyone knows what being "happy" is, right?—they are much too vague to be helpful in determining whether progress is being made. For this reason, the therapist helped Lee develop his answers into more specific, concrete, and behavioral signs of success.

> LEE (long pause): Maybe work wouldn't be my entire life. Maybe, like I said, I would start living my life again. You know, I got this great job and I haven't done anything for myself since.
> TH: So after this miracle, then, you would be doing more things for yourself?
> LEE: Yeah. I would.
> TH: Like what? What would you be doing for yourself?

LEE: Well, I've always toyed with the idea of making my little photography hobby into a, you know, small business. I take pictures of professional sporting events like car races and skiing and such.

TH: Uh-huh. What else would tell you that you were doing more things for yourself?

LEE: Well, I know my bosses won't like this, but maybe I would leave work on time for once.

TH: Leave work on time?

LEE: Yeah. I have this habit of staying after work and making up for the mistakes that my guys have made.

TH: And so after the miracle you would—

LEE: I would—I would let them be responsible for themselves. I wouldn't clean up their messes.

TH: How would that make a difference for you?

LEE: Well, they would have to be responsible and I could get home at a reasonable time instead of staying until all hours of the night. Then I get all bent out of shape.

TH: So what would you do different then?

LEE: Well, if I let them be responsible, maybe I wouldn't be so keyed up when I finally left work. Maybe then I wouldn't need to stop by the bar, bitch and complain to Ted, and drink my frustrations away.

❑

The therapist continued for a while longer, helping Lee define his desired outcome in even more specific, concrete, and behavioral terms. As you can see from this short excerpt, however, Lee was already defining his miracle in a way that pointed to some things he could immediately begin doing differently in order to solve his problem. In addition, such specific statements would enable him to make clear judgments about whether he was making progress or not. The therapist continued for several more minutes, helping Lee to be even more specific.

Being specific, concrete, and behavioral in your response to the miracle question is one of the most important keys you can have for opening the door to solution. Take the time to review your answers before moving on to the next key.

KEY 4: BE SURE YOU STATE WHAT YOU *WILL* DO RATHER THAN WHAT YOU *WON'T* DO.

Try a little experiment. When you read this sentence, *don't* think about Mickey Mouse! Can you do it? Come on now, don't think about him. Don't think about that cute little mouse with those big black ears and that high voice. Whatever you do, don't think about Mickey Mouse's girl friend's name right now. Just ignore that altogether. Please don't even let the name of that *minnie-ature* creature come into your mind. Can you do it? Of course not. Yet this is precisely the way that the majority of popular alcohol programs operate—that is, they talk about what you are *not* supposed to do!

In our work with homeless men who have alcohol problems, we have learned that one of the times they are most prone to have setbacks is directly after attending a recovery-oriented meeting. In contrast with what one might hope—that people with alcohol problems receive the support and direction that they need in order to overcome their problems—attendance at recovery-oriented meetings often triggers the very thing it is supposed to help stop. Why? The answer is simple. These meetings focus on achieving the impossible: *not* doing something! In this case the something that everyone attending such meetings is trying not to do is drink. As our little experiment demonstrates, however, it is not possible not to do something. As humans we are always in a state of doing something—even when we say that the something we are doing is "nothing." Constant thinking about what we are not supposed to think about or do has the effect of keeping the forbidden activity or thought in our minds. Having a thought repeat over and over in our minds increases the likelihood that we will act on that thought. Hence the problem drinking that we see in our homeless male clients following recovery-oriented meetings.

What is the solution? you may ask. As you describe your miracle, focus on what you do want rather than on what you don't want. Don't tell yourself not to think about or not to do something—drink alcohol, for instance. Rather, tell yourself to think about something else. Oftentimes, when we ask clients what they want in their miracles, they answer with what they don't want or no longer want. A person with a drinking problem, for example, may say that he or she no longer wants to have an alcohol problem. Similarly, the partner of a problem drinker may say that he or she does not want the spouse to drink or spend money on alcohol or to drive the family car while intoxicated. As you can see, however, these statements do not tell us what the person *does* want.

Making what you don't want to have in your life the focus of your efforts will make it more difficult to achieve success in the long run. Why? Well, when you are trying not to do something, it becomes difficult, if not impossible, to tell when you have succeeded. At what point do you consider yourself successful? After all, the problem behavior may happen again. This is precisely why traditional treatment professionals say that recovery is a lifelong process. If your goal is not to do something—like drinking—then you can never be finished with the treatment because the problem may recur at any time. This is also why such experts issue the warning that "a slip can occur at any time" as a standard part of their treatment procedures. And what does it mean if the problem behavior recurs when your objective is not to do something? If you think like a traditional recovery-oriented person, you are forced to start over from the very beginning.

This type of perfectionistic thinking is not only nonsensical but downright dangerous to the person struggling to overcome an alcohol problem. Furthermore, describing the failures that clients experience, while trying to live up to these impossibly high standards, as an inevitable part of the recovery process in no way excuses traditional treatment professionals from the responsibility of doing something to help prevent them.

By stating what you will be doing rather than what you won't be doing after the miracle, you will be able both to recognize your success and to determine what else remains to be accomplished. Therefore, whenever you find yourself using words such as *no, never, don't, won't, can't, wouldn't,* or *shouldn't* to describe your miracle, substitute the words *yes, when, do, will, can, would,* and *should.* Be careful not to let the negative words—what we call N words—creep into your description through the back door. For example, saying that you *should* abstain from alcohol is still negatively stated. To get around this, you can ask yourself, "What shall I be doing instead of drinking?"

❑

BACK TO THE DOCKS

As a way of illustrating this key, let us return to the case of Lee. You will recall that a large number of the responses that Lee gave to the "miracle" question were stated in negative terms. For example, among other things, he said that he would *not* be talking negatively all the time, he would *not* have a "wrinkled brow and knotted-up forehead," he would *not* hide from his employees, he would *not* stop by his favorite bar and complain to the bartender, Ted. Allowing Lee's responses to remain in such negatively stated terms would, as we have pointed out, increase his chances of failure. The therapist spent considerable time helping Lee turn his evolving description into more positive, proactive terms. Here is a sample of some of the dialogue starting where the last excerpt left off:

LEE: Well, if I let them be responsible, maybe I wouldn't be so keyed up when I finally left work. Maybe then I wouldn't need to stop by the bar, bitch and complain to Ted, and drink my frustrations away.

TH: So you wouldn't stop by the bar?

LEE: Right.

TH: What would you do instead?

LEE: Well, like I said earlier, I have this photography hobby that I've played around with for years, so . . . maybe I'd start doing some of that during the evenings. You know, preparing and stuff.

TH: Uh-huh. What else would you do instead of going to the bar?

LEE *(laughs):* Maybe I'd go on a date or something!

TH *(smiling):* You would! Tell me more about that.

At this point discussion about the miracle returned to the last key, with Lee and the therapist spending several minutes identifying in specific and concrete terms exactly what Lee would do on such a date. This included discussion about whom he might date as well as where he and his date might go and what they might do while together. After adding considerable detail to this aspect of the picture, the therapist brought the discussion back to some of the negatively stated responses that Lee had given earlier in response to the miracle.

TH: Lee, earlier you said a couple of things that I wanted to follow up on with you.

LEE: Okay, shoot.

TH: You said that after this miracle you wouldn't be hiding at work.

LEE: Yeah, that's right. [*Laughing.*] Right now, like I say, it's kind of like I have a magnetic butt and a steel chair or a steel butt and a magnetic chair.

TH *(laughs):* Uh-huh. So you've been stuck in that chair, I guess.

LEE: Yeah.

TH: So what will you do instead of staying stuck in your chair?

LEE: If this miracle were to happen?

TH: Yeah.

LEE: Well, I would be going around the loading dock like I used to. You know, talking to the guys, making sure that the work gets done and done right. [*Pause.*] I would reserve paper work and phone calls to the afternoon when my dock workers have knocked off for the day.

TH: Hmm. What else?

LEE: Well, I would start talking to management again. I used to walk through the office several times a day. Lately here, well, I've been trying to avoid them.

❑

Lee's miracle becomes more attainable the more he is able to describe what he *will* be doing rather than what he *won't* be doing. You may find it helpful to model your responses after Lee's. While we know that it can be difficult to state what you want in positive rather than negative terms, we promise that your effort will be rewarded. For this reason, take some time now to review your answers to the "miracle" question. Every time you find an N word or a statement about what you won't be doing after the miracle, be careful to turn your answer into something positive or into a statement about what you will be doing instead. To aid you in this process, here are some questions that we routinely ask our clients to help them describe their miracle in positive, proactive terms:

- When you are no longer (insert negative word here), what will you be doing instead?
- What will others see you doing differently when (insert negative word here) is no longer happening?
- When (insert negative work here) is no longer happening, what will be happening instead?
- What will others notice different about you when (insert negative word here) is no longer happening?

- How will you know when (insert negative word here) has stopped and the miracle has started? What will you see that is different?
- What will be the first small sign that (insert negative word here) is getting better?

If you are still having difficulty stating what you will do or what will be happening rather than what you won't do or what won't be happening, consider answering these questions:

- When you are no longer (insert negative word here), what will you not be doing then?
- What will you be doing instead of those things?

KEY 5: STATE HOW YOU WILL START YOUR JOURNEY RATHER THAN HOW YOU WILL END IT.

You have probably heard the old saying "A journey of a thousand miles begins with one step." What this means is that no matter how large or insurmountable something seems, it can be accomplished if you focus on taking the first few steps rather than on the eventual outcome.

Similarly, you are much more likely to be successful in reaching your desired destination if you pay extraclose attention to the first few steps of your journey. Focusing on the initial steps of the pathway to solution rather than on the eventual solution itself helps you maintain the hope and motivation you need to continue your day-to-day efforts to solve your problem. This only stands to reason. If you are always focused on the eventual outcome, you will be less likely to recognize the progress you are making along the way. If you don't recognize your progress, you are not going to nurture these small changes into the lasting solutions that you desire.

Often clients initially describe their miracles in completed forms. In other words, they talk about the end results they hope to achieve. For example, they may say that the miracle is that they will be happy and sober, have good marriages, or enjoy better sex lives. Such descriptions indicate that these people are able to envision the possibility of life's being somehow different, but, they are likely to remain only possibilities unless time is taken to define how the first few steps toward those possibilities look. In this regard, our clients have found the following questions useful for depicting their miracles in terms of the start rather than the end of something:

• How will you know that the miracle has started?
• As you open your eyes tomorrow morning, what will be the first sign that the miracle has happened?
• Who would be the first person to notice that the miracle is happening, and what would that person say that he or she would notice first?
• On a scale from 1 to 10, in which 10 is the day after the miracle and 1 is where you are today, what will be the first thing you will notice that will tell you that you are moving up the scale?

□

THE FOREMAN'S FIRST STEPS

Returning once again to the case we have been presenting throughout this chapter, the therapist helped the foreman state what his first steps would be by asking him a scaling question.

TH: Lee, on a scale from one to ten, in which ten is the day after the miracle and one is where you are today, what would be one small step that would tell you that you have moved up the scale? Say, to a two on the scale?
LEE: A two, eh? [Pause]
TH: Yeah, a two. Not a three or four. Just a two. What would that look like?

LEE: Something small then, right?

[Therapist nods affirmatively.]

LEE: Well, if I could just wear a smile on my face tomorrow, you know, maybe say hello to the guys when I come in.

TH: Would they notice that?

LEE: Oh, yes, they would notice that. Yeah, they would probably wonder what's up. They might think that something was wrong. Maybe think that I knew something I wasn't supposed to know and that they were in trouble or something.

❑

Lee's idea about smiling was a small, first step; more important, it was something that he could actually do his next day on the job. Before moving on to the next and last key, review your answers to the "miracle" question, and be sure they indicate how the first few steps on your journey toward solution will look.

KEY 6: BE CLEAR ABOUT WHO, WHERE, AND WHEN, BUT NOT WHY.

There is an old story about a young scientist from the United States who challenged the teachings of an Indian guru. "You believe," the young scientist asked the guru in a sarcastic tone of voice, "that the world rests on the backs of two elephants?" The guru nodded and, in a quiet voice, said, "I do." Sensing an opportunity to prove the superiority of Western thinking, the young scientist then asked, "Then what, might I ask, do those elephants stand on?" Matter-of-factly the guru responded that these elephants stood on the backs of yet two more elephants. When the young scientist started to ask what these elephants in turn stood on, the guru raised his hand to interrupt him and said, "It is of no use to question further. It is elephants all the way down!"

The same point made by the guru was made in an interaction we once watched between a student and a counselor who was well known for his successful clinical work with problem drinkers. The student asked the counselor why people continued to drink when doing so caused them and their families so much pain and heartache. The wise counselor thought momentarily and then responded, "Because they keep putting the bottle to their lips and swallowing!"

Anyone who has reared a child knows what the Indian guru and wise counselor meant by their answers. There simply is no final answer to the question of why, since any answer that is given can be followed by another question of why. And we have observed that the most obvious result of such questioning is inaction. In other words, while trying to figure out the cause of something, one is less likely to take any action to try to change it. As we have already indicated, however, one does not need to understand the cause of something in order to change it. To the contrary, the process of change begins by specifying exactly how one would like things to be different. Three important details in this regard are the who, where, and when—not the why—of the desired change.

With regard to the who, our clients have found it helpful to consider the details of the desired change from the perspectives of the important people in their lives. These typically include spouses, children, parents, employers, and friends. These significant others are often greatly affected by our clients' alcohol use. What is more important, however, is that they are also affected when our clients solve their problems, such as when our clients no longer have a problem with alcohol. For this reason, we encourage our clients to speculate on two different things once they have solved their problems: what their significant others will notice is different about them and what they will notice is different about their significant others. Two potential side effects of such thinking are that many of our clients experience an increased sense of hopefulness about the future and discover vital clues to solving their problems.

Traditional treatment professionals have long recognized that alcohol problems affect more than the users. Despite this awareness, however, families, friends, loved ones, and employers have traditionally been excluded from the treatment process. People affected by others' problems with alcohol have typically been relegated to a role of helping their loved ones get into some form of treatment. After that they are sent to their own treatment and support groups separate from the problem drinkers. In these groups they are most often taught how, despite their best intentions, they have actually contributed to the continuation of the problem. They are labeled "enablers" and "codependents," told that they are "out of touch with reality and suffering from essentially the same disease" as the problem drinkers, and encouraged to begin their own separate programs of recovery.[9]

Our successful clients, on the other hand, uniformly incorporate the perspectives of their significant others into their pictures of success and personal plans of recovery. Here are some questions that our clients have found useful in helping them do this:

- Who will be the first person to notice that the miracle has happened? What will that person notice?
- What will your (spouse, children, friends, employer) notice is different about you after the miracle?
- What will you notice is different about your (spouse, children, friends, employer) after the miracle?
- Who will be most surprised when your problem is solved? What will that person see you doing that he or she would never have thought possible? What will you see that person doing different that you would never have thought possible?

After considering the who, take time to consider the where and when of your solution. The traditional view notwithstanding, alcohol problems do not pervade every aspect of a person's life. Indeed, we have observed that most clients have times when, as well as places where, they do not use alcohol. Most traditional treatment approaches ignore such instances. Problem drinking is viewed instead as present in every aspect of a person's life. Even when a person is not using, he or she is said to exhibit the personality flaws that characterize people with alcohol problems.

In developing a solution, we have found it extremely helpful to specify exactly where and when the solution is most likely to occur.

❑

CALVIN COOLS IT

Take, for instance, Calvin, a forty-five-year-old engineer who came for treatment of a serious problem with crack cocaine. Calvin had recently experienced a close brush with death when he suffered a heart attack following an evening of heavy cocaine smoking. Understandably the incident frightened him greatly, and he expressed a strong desire to quit using crack. He said, however, that he didn't have much hope about being able to quit because he had already failed two drug treatment programs. Over the course of the interview we learned that Calvin was the most tempted to smoke crack when he got paid. Indeed, on the night of his heart attack Calvin had smoked up his entire month's paycheck in just a few hours. Part of the solution that Calvin eventually developed was to have his checks directly deposited in his bank. He told us that when he did not have the money in his hands, he was better able to withstand the strong urges to use crack. He combined this strategy with plans to engage in social outings with friends from work each payday.

Calvin's story is a perfect example of the benefits of specifying the where and when of the solution. Calvin was most likely to succeed *when* he did not have money in his hands.

Where was Calvin most likely to succeed? With friends from work. Calvin's successful treatment largely amounted to helping him identify and then repeat these patterns.

❑

You, too, can benefit by being specific about the where and when of your solution by answering the following questions:

- Where are you most likely to be when you first notice that the miracle has happened? What will you be most likely to notice?
- Where are you most likely to be successful in (specify desired change here)?
- Where would others say you are most likely to be successful?
- Where have you been successful in the past?
- Where would others say you have been successful in the past?
- When have you been successful in the past? What was different that caused you to be successful?
- When would others say you have been successful? What would they say caused you to be successful then?
- Where would you guarantee that you would not be successful? Where would you guarantee that you would?

DISCOVERING THE RIGHT SET OF KEYS FOR YOU

On the old television game show "Split Second" contestants competed with each other to answer a series of difficult questions. The contestant answering the most questions by the end of the game received the opportunity to win a brand-new automobile. All he or she had to do was pick the right key—the one that started the car—from a group of similar-looking keys. If the key the contestant chose happened to start the car, then he or she won the car, was retired as a champion, and quickly faded into television history. If the key did not start the car, the contestant was invited to return for another chance on the next day's show. Of course, the contestant once again had to go through all the hard work of answering the questions in order to win another chance at the car.

In some ways unlocking your door to solution is like being a contestant on "Split Second." You may have to try several different keys or combinations of keys before you are successful. Don't give up! Success requires hard work and determination. Give yourself credit for the hard work you are doing to solve your problem, however small or insignificant the changes may seem. Small changes will not grow into the bigger, lasting changes you desire if they are not noticed and nurtured along the way. Be realistic in your expectations for progress. The problem that you are struggling with is not easy to solve. If it were as easy as, for example, "Just say no," then you would have already solved it by now!

We hope that our being up front about the hard work involved in solving your alcohol problem will forestall any chances of your becoming disappointed and giving up when you try to implement the advice in this chapter. In theory the ideas are simple; in practice, however, they are not easy. Indeed, over the years we have learned that there is a vast difference between simple and easy. Trying to put these simple ideas into practice will most likely be some of the hardest work of your life. Putting them into practice is possible, however. We know, because we help people put these ideas into practice every day in our clinical work with problem drinkers. Like us, you will probably experience some successes and some failures. Pay close attention to your successes, and don't give in to the temptation of continuing to try something that doesn't work for you. If you need a booster during the process, refer to the "Miracle" Method Ready Reference.

❑

SUCCESS "ON THE DOCKS"

One final note about Lee. Toward the conclusion of the first interview he and the therapist worked hard to identify the "who, where, and when" of his miracle and then scheduled a session for the following week. When he returned for his second session, Lee reported that he had worn a smile to work each day. "The first day," he told the therapist, "was the most difficult." This difficulty soon evaporated, he told the therapist, when, as he had predicted, his smile began to unnerve some of the employees on the loading platform. Fearing that Lee was wise to them, they stopped playing games and began working hard once again. This, of course, affected Lee. He had not visited the bar all week.

THE MIRACLE METHOD
READY REFERENCE
❑

Finding the door to solution begins with the choice: I want my life to be different!

Opening the door to solution begins with considering how you want your life to be different once your problem is solved: Suppose a miracle happened . . .

Unlocking the door to solution is accomplished with the six keys:

1. Make sure your miracle is important to you.
2. Keep it small.
3. Make it specific, concrete, and behavioral.
4. Be sure you state what you *will* do rather than what you *won't* do.
5. State how you will start your journey rather than how you will end it.
6. Be clear about who, where, and when, but not why.

4

Lessons from Oz

THREE VALUABLE CLUES FOR FINDING
YOUR WAY ALONG THE PATH TO SOLUTION

So often times it happens,
That we live our lives in chains,
And we never even know,
We have the key.
                    —J. Tempchin and R. Stradlund,
                                "Already Gone"

. . . the kingdom of God is within you.
                                —Luke 17:21

The Wizard of Oz was, by his own admission, "a very poor wizard." He was, however, a marvelous therapist. Take a moment to ponder the classic movie. The Scarecrow, the Lion, the Tin Woodsman, and Dorothy all approach the Wizard believing that they are lacking some ability or quality. The clumsy Scarecrow needs a brain, the frightened Lion lacks courage, and the hollow Tin Woodsman is missing a heart. Dorothy, you will recall, believes that she lacks the power to return home to her loved ones. What does the Wizard propose to help this motley crew? He sends them on a journey. This journey seems to have little to do with what the members of the group are asking him to help them with; furthermore, it is fraught with danger. For example, the group must deal with flying monkeys, traverse the steep cliffs leading up to the Wicked Witch's castle, manage to sneak by the palace guards—not to mention confront the Wicked Witch and somehow obtain her broom. In response to their pleas for help, the great and powerful Wizard of Oz simply tells the group to get on with their journey!

What is therapeutic about this? you may be wondering. Well, along the way all the group members discover that they already possess the quality they are asking the Wizard to give them. The Scarecrow uses his brain to develop a plan to outwit the guards and gain entrance to the castle of the Wicked Witch of the West. The cowardly Lion braves the rocky slope leading up to the castle and fights off the guards. The Woodsman displays the deep feelings of commitment he has toward his friends.

Strange as it may seem, the story of the Wizard of Oz is very similar to how people change in solution-focused therapy. Clients go on a journey of sorts on which they discover that they already possess what they thought only the wizard-therapist could give them: the solution to their problems! In other words, solution-focused therapists help their clients discover the skills, strengths, and solutions that they already possess but may not recognize or know how to use to their advantage.

Traditionally, treatment professionals spend very little time identifying and using these strengths, resources, and solutions. Indeed, in the field of alcohol treatment these client resources have not only been ignored but often viewed with suspicion—and sometimes even labeled dangerous. Take as one example problem drinkers who have somehow managed either to stop or to control their drinking on their own. "Don't be fooled by prolonged periods of non-problem use of alcohol," the experts counsel. *"You are not capable of controlling your drinking! You are powerless over alcohol!"*[1] "There may be plateaus . . . but the disease moves inexorably toward greater and more serious deterioration over time. . . . Left unchecked," says recovery guru Vernon Johnson, "chemical dependency is a 100 percent fatal disease."[2]

Problem drinkers are routinely portrayed as defensive, sneaky, and manipulative. For this reason, professionals and family members are counseled by the so-called alcoholism treatment experts not to be fooled by any "good" behavior on the part of a problem drinker. The "disease of alcoholism," they tell us, is tricky. "A single slip can precipitate a return to the active stages of the disease," says Johnson. In this way, prolonged periods of sobriety are labeled "dry drunks" rather than "critical first steps toward success"; relapses and setbacks are viewed as evidence of the progressive disease of alcoholism rather than as a part of any attempt to change one's behavior; and so on. The primary focus of most traditional treatment is locating the weaknesses, deficits, and problems that the client brings into therapy. The fact is, however, that the *client's own resources may be responsible for as much as three-fifths (60 percent) of any change seen in treatment.*[3]

The exclusive emphasis in traditional treatment on weakness was demonstrated in a recent interaction we had with the administrator of a community mental health and substance abuse agency. After we had conducted a workshop for the agency staff, the administrator asked us to look over the forms that the workers use to gather information about clients prior to treatment. Five pages of information were collected about each client's problem. Out of these five pages, however, only one line—a single line—at the bottom of the last page asked the therapist to state any client strengths.

BUT DON'T THERAPISTS HAVE THE SOLUTIONS?

Now, you might reasonably ask, why force clients to discover their own solutions? Why send them on a journey that can be fraught with danger and has the potential, as is the case in *The Wizard of Oz,* for failure? Don't therapists know the best solutions? Why don't they just point out the best solutions to their clients? Wouldn't that be easier and more efficient?

The answer is that it would indeed be much easier and more efficient. The problem is, however, that this approach just doesn't work. Once again we can learn from the story of *The Wizard of Oz*. Think back again to the movie. In particular, recall what takes place when the Wizard tries to solve Dorothy's problem for her by flying her back to Kansas in a hot-air balloon. He not only fails at his task but leaves her stranded and heartbroken in the Land of Oz. The day is saved only when Glenda, the Good Witch, shows up and informs Dorothy that she doesn't need the Wizard to get back to Kansas because she herself has always possessed the power to go home. All she needs to do, according to Glenda, is to click the ruby slippers together three times in rapid succession while repeating the phrase "There's no place like home."

In the closing moments of the film the Good Witch tells us why it doesn't work for therapists to tell clients about the solutions they already possess but do not recognize. She does so in response to a question from the Scarecrow, who wonders why Dorothy wasn't simply told at the outset of her journey that she possessed the power to return home. Wisely Glenda responds, "Because she [Dorothy] wouldn't have believed me . . . *she had to learn it for herself.*"

You started your own journey toward solution when you began reading this book. In the previous chapter you mapped out what you wanted to accomplish on your journey as you answered the "miracle" question. In this chapter you will learn three specific clues to find the skills, strengths, and solutions you already possess but may not recognize or know how to use to your advantage. Don't be surprised if these clues lead you to conclude what the Wizard of Oz knew all along: that you have always possessed the exact thing you thought you didn't have, the solution to your problem.

THREE CLUES TO SOLUTION

CLUE 1: LOOK FOR PIECES OF THE MIRACLE THAT ARE HAPPENING NOW.

There is a well-known joke about a police officer who happens on a drunk who is crawling around on his hands and knees under a streetlamp. When the policeman asks the man why he is crawling around on all fours, the man replies that he is looking for his keys, which, he says, pointing off into the darkness, he lost somewhere "over there." Confused by the man's answer, the police officer asks, "But why on earth would you look here under the streetlamp if, as you say, you lost your keys *over there?*"

"Why, because," the intoxicated man responds matter-of-factly, "it's too dark to look *over there!*"

Problem drinkers are often like the man searching for his lost keys under the streetlamp. They search in the most illuminated but frequently the least obvious places where the solution may be present. Most of their time is spent, for example, studying, analyzing, talking about, and trying to understand the problem rather than looking for, noticing, and utilizing solutions that already exist. That we all do this makes some sense, since the problem is typically foremost in our minds. However, while the problem often occupies center stage in our awareness, it is clearly not the most obvious place to look for solutions. As in the story of the man under the streetlamp, the most obvious place to look for the solution is where it already exists—in other words, the place where and when solutions may already be happening but, for some reason or another, have gone unrecognized or even been dismissed as flukes.

How can you find these solutions that already exist? First, take a moment to think back on the work you completed in the last chapter. You were asked to imagine and then describe in detail how your life would be different once your problem was solved. Well, the search for existing solutions starts right there with your description. Specifically the search starts by reviewing your description and then *looking for times when pieces of what you described are already happening in your life or have happened in the past.* Such times are known as *instances*[4]—in other words, instances of the miracle occurring in your life in the recent past or in the present.

We have found that helping our clients first notice and then later examine those times when pieces of the miracle are already happening in their lives serves two purposes. First it brings existing solutions into awareness; then it enables clients to repeat those solutions in the future. Philosophers argue over whether a noise is made when a tree falls in the forest and no one is around to hear it. Whatever the philosophers eventually decide, we know that solutions that are not noticed will not make a noise—a difference, in other words—and will eventually disappear. For this reason, you must be diligent in examining your experience for evidence of existing solutions.

Therefore, before reading any further, take some time to review your answers to the miracle question and look for instances. As you review your answers, consider the following questions:

- When was the most recent time that even a small piece of this miracle was happening?
- What would others say was the most recent time that even a small piece of the miracle happened?
- When in your lifetime have you experienced even a small piece of the miracle you describe?
- When in your lifetime would others say you have experienced even a small piece of this miracle you describe?

❏

DOWN AND OUT AND NOT IN BEVERLY HILLS

Russell was a financial planner who was down on his luck.
During the 1980s he lived with his wife and two children in a
luxurious house in Beverly Hills. A combination of alcohol and
poor investment decisions, however, cost him his family and
business. Discouraged, depressed, and broke, Russell was
eventually forced to leave California and return to the Midwest
to live with his folks. When we met him for the first time, he
had been back just two weeks.

Initially Russell stated that there was no hope for him and
that he would probably be better off dead. There was nothing
left for him in this life: He had lost his job, his home, his wife,
and his children. Eventually we asked Russell the miracle
question. Among other things he talked about being sober,
maintaining contact with his children, and finding work. When
we asked him to describe in more detail what he meant when
he said he would be "sober," a smile crept onto his face for the
first time during the session. "You know," he said, "I guess it
would mean that I would be more like I have been for the last
two weeks." When we asked him to explain, he told us that he
had not had a drink since moving in with his parents.

Russell's experience is not uncommon. When we ask them
the question, problem drinkers are frequently able to recall
periods in which pieces of their miracle have happened in their
lives. Noticing such instances is the first step toward being able
to repeat them in the future.

❏

Putting the Pieces of the Puzzle Together

Noticing that you have experienced times when pieces of the miracle have happened is only the first step toward using Clue 1 to solve your problem. In order to repeat such change in the future, you need to gather more information, specifically information that may lead you to an understanding of what is different about the times you experience a piece of the miracle. Think about the pattern of events surrounding those times. Looking for patterns in the history of your experiences is, as you may recognize, very similar to what takes place in most traditional treatment. The major difference is that in traditional treatment you are asked to go into detail about the patterns and events surrounding *the problem,* with the intention of understanding and thereby being able to change or eliminate such patterns. In solution-focused treatment, however, you are helped to discover the patterns surrounding *the solutions,* with the hope that such patterns can be strengthened and encouraged to recur.

The following questions are intended to help you gain an understanding of the circumstances and patterns surrounding the times when pieces of the miracle occur. Discovering these patterns is the key to being deliberately able to repeat the pieces of the miracle in the future. Specifically the questions focus on what we call the what, where, who, when, and how of the events you have experienced:

- **What . . .**
  . . . did you notice yourself doing differently when you experienced the pieces of the miracle?
  . . . did others see you doing when you experienced these changes? What exactly did they see you doing that told them you had experienced a change?
  . . . was happening shortly before and after you experienced the pieces of the miracle? What else? How did this influence the occurrence of pieces of the miracle?
  . . . (would/do) others say was happening shortly before

and after you experienced the pieces of the miracle? What
else? How did this influence the occurrence of pieces of
the miracle?

. . . did you do to bring about the occurrence of the pieces
of the miracle, either in whole or in part?

. . . weren't you doing at the time you experienced the
pieces of the miracle that might have caused them to
happen? What were you doing instead? How did this
influence their occurrence?

. . . would (you/others) have to see you doing again to
convince (you/them) that the occurrences of these pieces
represent the beginning of a real miracle, not just a fluke?

• **Where . . .**

. . . were you when the pieces of the miracle happened?
How (or) did this influence their occurrence?

. . . were you shortly before or after the pieces of the
miracle happened? How did this influence their
occurrence?

. . . *hadn't* you been either before, after, or while these
pieces were happening that might have played a role in
their occurrence? Where were you instead?

• **Who . . .**

. . . *was* around when you experienced the pieces of the
miracle? How did this influence the occurrence of pieces
of the miracle?

. . . was *not* around when you experienced the pieces of
the miracle? How did this influence their occurrence?

• **When . . .**

. . . did the pieces of the miracle occur? What role do the
time of day, day of the week, week of the month, etc. play
in the occurrence of pieces of the miracle?

• **How . . .**

. . . did you make the pieces of the miracle happen? What
specifically did you do differently that caused the change
to happen?

. . . did others cause the pieces of the miracle to come about? What specifically did these others do that influenced the occurrence of pieces of the miracle?

❑

"BEVERLY HILLS 90210": REVISITED

When Russell told the therapist that he was experiencing an instance of the miracle he was describing, the therapist began to ask him the who, what, when, where, and how questions. This was done in an attempt to learn more about the pattern of events surrounding the instance so that Russell could repeat his success in the future. Here is a excerpt of the dialogue from that part of session:

THERAPIST: You say you haven't had a drink since moving in with your parents?

RUSSELL: That's right. Last drink I had was . . . twelve days ago. Tonight at midnight will be my thirteenth day of abstinence.

TH: Congratulations.

RUSSELL: Thank you.

TH: *How* have you done it?

RUSSELL: It has ruined my whole life, and I'm tired of it. I've lost my family and everything.

TH: Yeah, I know, but *how* did you turn those feelings into action?

RUSSELL: My parents have been helpful.

TH: What have your parents done that has helped you experience this success?

RUSSELL: Well, for one thing, they told me they would help me see my kids.

TH: That helped?

RUSSELL: Yeah.

TH: *How* did it help to know that you will be seeing you kids?

RUSSELL: Well, it's like something to shoot for. They told me that they would help me see my kids if I didn't drink.

TH: I see. You must really love your kids.

RUSSELL: I do.

TH: *What* do you do to keep your kids in mind? Because I'm sure you've had temptations, right?

RUSSELL: Oh, yes. Just last night I felt like going out and getting something to drink but I didn't.

TH *(surprised)*: You didn't. *What* did you do instead?

RUSSELL: I called and talked with my kids.

TH: Wow. *Where* did you get that idea?

RUSSELL: It was tough, too, because it's so hard with them so far away.

TH: Sure. *What* was helpful about talking with your kids?

RUSSELL *(tearful)*: They told me they loved me and missed me.

TH: That helped?

RUSSELL: Oh, yeah, it helped a lot. I think there's hope then. You know, since they love me and miss me, that means they aren't forgetting me. That means that I matter to someone, to them.

TH: And that helps. Anything else that you can think of that may have helped bring about these nearly thirteen days of success?

□

As you can see from this brief excerpt, Russell had started to identify elements of the pattern surrounding his thirteen days of sobriety. Obviously, doing things that help him keep his children in mind will help him continue his success. Russell and the therapist continued to explore the pattern of events surrounding his success for several more minutes.

Before reading on, take some time to review your answer to the miracle question, and look for evidence of instances. So that you will not misunderstand this last example, let us state our point clearly: Unlike Russell's your instances of success do not have to be related to your drinking problem. Simply look for times when you have experienced pieces of your miracle.

CLUE 2: LEARN FROM YOUR LACK OF MISTAKES.

In one of our favorite Sherlock Holmes stories the famous detective is called in after Scotland Yard detectives have failed to solve a mystery involving the disappearance of the valuable racehorse Silver Blaze.[5] We learn from Holmes's companion and sidekick Dr. Watson that the horse vanished from its stall just days before the biggest race of the season and that the owner stands to lose a considerable sum of money should it not be found before the race is run. As is true of all cases involving Holmes, there are many suspects and few, if any, real clues. To the surprise of everyone—everyone but the reader, of course— Holmes quickly solves the case, finding the horse and identifying the guilty party.

How, you might ask, does Holmes succeed where everyone else has failed? Why, of course, by noticing a critical clue that everyone else in the case has overlooked. That the clue escapes the notice of everyone but Sherlock Holmes is not all that surprising, however, since the ever-observant master detective manages to notice the impossible: He notices something that did *not* happen. In particular, he notices that the stable keepers' dog did *not* bark when the thief entered the livery to steal Silver Blaze. This "curious incident," as Holmes refers to the clue, shows that the dog *knew* the person who stole the horse. Once Holmes notices this nonincident, the identity of the thief becomes obvious and the case is solved.

Noticing, as Holmes does, when things do *not* happen is not easy. Indeed, after reviewing the available research on the topic from the field of human perception, the psychologists Richard N. Nisbett and Lee R. Ross conclude that it is nearly impossible.[6] As a species we experience considerable difficulty noticing and therefore appreciating the value of such information. As we see in the story of "Silver Blaze," however, such "null information," as researchers call it, may provide valuable clues to the solution of difficult and perplexing problems.

This is particularly true in attempts to find solutions to such difficult personal problems as problem drinking. We have found, for example, that null information—that is, those times when a person either does not drink or does not have a drinking problem—is often extremely helpful in providing clues to the solution of his alcohol problem. Indeed, the periods are so important that we have even given them a special name: *exceptions*. Simply stated, exceptions are those times when people do not experience their usual pattern of problem drinking. For example, a person may stop drinking completely, drink in more a responsible and controlled fashion, become involved in a recovery or other treatment program, or change his or her use of alcohol in some other beneficial way. In short, the person does not display the usual pattern of problem drinking that is troublesome.

Consider Ralph, a man we first met in the hospital where he was receiving medical treatment after nearly dying from a two-month-long binge on alcohol. Ralph had a long history of problem drinking that had landed him in the hospital on more than one occasion. We were supposed to determine whether or not he should be referred to a twenty-eight-day inpatient program for the treatment of his alcohol problem. As part of our standard solution-focused assessment, we asked Ralph to tell us about the last time he was sober. Given our experience with exceptions, we were not surprised when he reported having been sober at periods during his life. We were surprised, however, when he told us that the most recent period had lasted *twelve years*! Needless to say, Ralph was not referred to the inpatient treatment program. Rather, during a handful of outpatient visits we explored what he had been doing to remain sober during his twelve-year exception period and then helped him develop a plan to carry out the same activities in the future.

Not all problem drinkers have experienced exception periods as long as Ralph's. However, in our work with problem drinkers we have found that the majority do experience times when their drinking is not a problem. For some, these exception periods have lasted for days, weeks, or even months. For others, however, the exceptions have occurred only briefly or in extremely special circumstances, such as being in a hospital or treatment program. Whatever the case, what is most crucial in using exceptions as clues to solving problem drinking is that the nonproblem periods be noticed and explored.

Curiously, few people notice or recognize the value of such periods in solving their problems. Indeed, such times are often considered accidents or flukes and dismissed by both problem drinkers and traditional treatment professionals. Nothing could be further from the truth. There is at least as much to be learned about solving a drinking problem from one's lack of mistakes as there is from one's mistakes. For this reason, it is important that you take time now to identify, think about, describe, and analyze those periods of time—however small or whatever the circumstances—when you do not experience your problem. The following instructions will aid you in the process of uncovering and utilizing your exceptions.

Beginning Your Search for Exceptions

On the line below draw a line at the point which indicates the percentage of time that drinking *is* a problem for you:

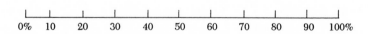

| 0% | 10 | 20 | 30 | 40 | 50 | 60 | 70 | 80 | 90 | 100% |

Now subtract from 100 the percentage of time that drinking is a problem for you. The result represents your exception periods. In other words, this is the percentage of time that you somehow manage not to have a problem with alcohol. For example, if you indicated that alcohol was a problem for you 70 percent of the time, subtracting this number from 100 percent means that 30 percent of the time you are successful in managing your drinking. If you indicated that drinking is a problem for you 100 percent of the time, you may want to rethink your answer before continuing. Few people always have problems with alcohol and fewer still drink all the time. Most people experience *some* times either when they do not drink or when they drink more normally. Never mind that the reason for not drinking may not seem acceptable to you at this time (e.g., you ran out of money, you were in jail or prison, you were in an inpatient detoxification or treatment program, your spouse threatened to leave you, your boss indicated that your job was at risk.

Identifying and Amplifying Your Exception Period Patterns

Take time to describe in detail the circumstances surrounding those times when you do not experience your problem. At this point in the process, include everything that occurs to you. This is not the time to edit or be critical of your responses. The more information you generate, the better. Each new piece of information increases the chances that in the future you will be able to repeat such periods deliberately. For this reason, be sure to include information about the situation, times, people, and places occurring before, during, and after you experience an exception period. You may find it helpful to imagine that you have a videotape of yourself during an exception period and then answer the following what, where, who, when, and how questions:

- **What . . .**
   . . . is different about those times when you are not having a drinking problem?

. . . are you doing differently during those times when you experience an exception?

. . . would others say you are doing differently during those times when you are able not to have a problem with alcohol?

. . . happens shortly before and after these times? How do these events influence the occurrence of an exception?

. . . would others say happens shortly before and after you experience an exception?

. . . thoughts, feelings, and behaviors occur just prior to and during an exception period? How are these related to the occurrence of an exception?

. . . aren't you doing at the time you experience an exception that might cause the change to happen? What are you doing instead?

• **Where . . .**

. . . are you when you are most likely to experience an exception? How is being there related to your not drinking problematically?

. . . are you shortly before or after these exception periods that might influence their occurrence?

. . . haven't you been before, after, or during these periods that might influence their occurrence?

• **Who . . .**

. . . is with you when you experience an exception?

. . . is not there when you experience an exception? How does being or not being around these people cause the exception to occur?

• **When . . .**

. . . are you most likely to experience an exception? What time of the day, day of the week, week of the month is it?

• **How . . .**

. . . do these exception periods come about?

. . . do others help bring about the exception periods?

What specifically do they do that contributes to the occurrence of an exception period?
. . . can you make these periods happen more often?

If You Are Still Clueless

Don't despair! As we indicated earlier, noticing when something is *not* happening is difficult. If you have tried but cannot recall any such times, you may find the following questions helpful in uncovering an exception that remains hidden. Even if you were fortunate enough to recall some exceptions to your problem, you will probably find these questions helpful in adding detail to your earlier answers. The questions work by focusing your attention on some successes you are likely to have had but are just as likely to have forgotten. You will get the most out of the questions if you first take a few minutes to think about times when you might have, should have, almost had, or even began to have a problem with alcohol but somehow managed to overcome, avoid, or deal with it in a way that was satisfactory to you. Once you have thought about these times, ask yourself these questions:

- How have you managed to overcome the urge or temptation to drink to the problem stage in the past? What did you actually *do* that helped you overcome the urge to drink at that time? What would others say you did?
- What exactly did you do the last time you thought you deserved a drink but decided not have one?
- What have you done in the past in order to stay out of situations in which the temptation to drink to excess might outweigh your resolve to stay sober?
- How have you managed to stop drinking to the point of its being a problem in the past? What did you actually *do* that finally helped you stop? What would others say you did?
- How did you manage to get back on track the last time you

experienced a setback in your efforts to solve your drinking problem?

• What was different about the last time you successfully managed to keep your drinking at an acceptable level to you and your loved ones? How did you do it? What would they say you did in order to be successful?

CLUE 3: LOOK FOR PRETREATMENT CHANGE.

In 1987 researchers Michele Weiner-Davis, Steve de Shazer, and Walter Gingrich decided to do a study on something that they had frequently observed in their work with clients but did not fully understand. If the truth be known, they were a little suspicious of it. Many of their clients came to the first treatment session reporting that since making the appointments for therapy, they had already made significant changes in their lives. Some of these clients had changed so significantly that they wondered whether or not they needed to be in treatment. Given their traditional training, the researchers were inclined to look upon such changes with suspicion. They had been trained to attribute any reports of change prior to the initiation of treatment to a host of negative qualities thought to characterize problem drinkers (e.g., resistance, denial). At the very least, they had been trained to minimize the significance of any such changes. The study, however, soon changed their perspective.

In order to conduct a systematic study of these clients, the researchers decided to ask their clients if they had experienced any changes for the better between the time they made their appointments for treatment and the first session of therapy. Fully two-thirds (66 percent) of these clients reported having experienced changes while awaiting their first appointments. Even more surprising, however, was that the majority of these clients considered such pretreatment changes important in solving the problems for which they were seeking help. In other words, the research showed that change occurring prior to the initiation of treatment was not only *not* uncommon but also *a significant part of the solution* to the client's problem.

The idea that a person with a drinking problem can change on his or her own either before or without the benefit of formal treatment is a radical one. You should be aware, therefore, that while the majority of problem drinkers are likely to experience pretreatment changes, most professional alcohol counselors are not likely to appreciate the value or relevance of such changes for the solution of alcohol problems. If you report such change, not only will you not get approval and reinforcement, but your report may even be interpreted as a sign of resistance or denial. You may be actively confronted and punished. This is probably due to the influence of the disease model, which holds, among other things, that problem drinkers cannot get better without formal treatment.[8]

The field of alcohol treatment has only recently been able to loosen itself from traditional thinking long enough to begin a systematic study of the significant percentage of problem drinkers who manage to overcome serious alcohol problems without the benefit of formal treatment. Preliminary data strongly suggest that there are substantial and consistent characteristics that enable certain individuals to overcome alcohol use problems without formal or lay treatment.[9] Learning how these people are successful will, we hope, influence alcohol treatment in the future. In the meantime, the individual problem drinker—you— can benefit from investigating any changes you make prior to the initiation of formal treatment and then incorporating those change-producing strategies into your personal plan for recovery.

If you have noticed a change in your problem prior to reading this book or have made any active attempt to solve your problem, then you may have begun to solve your problem. As was the case with the previous clues, however, such change needs to be noticed and nurtured if it is to have any beneficial impact on your problem. For this reason, before you read any further, take a few minutes to answer this question: "Many times, in between the time that a person decides to get some help for their problem and the time they actually take the first steps to solve that problem, they notice that things already seem better or different. What have you noticed about your situation?"[10]

Don't give up if you can't immediately think of any examples of pretreatment change in your own life. As you will recall, fully one-third of the clients in the research project were not able to think of any concrete examples of pretreatment change when the question was posed at the beginning of the session. You can take heart, however, in the finding that the clients who couldn't think of any changes for the better when initially asked were able to think of such times by the end of the meeting. The upshot of this is that you should really take some time to think over the past few weeks and look for any times when you experienced a change for the better.

❑

AGAINST ALL ODDS

Annette was a seventeen-year-old who came for treatment accompanied by her parents. According to her mother, Annette had been "a problem from the day she was born." She had been a difficult baby to care for and always seemed to be sick. She was always getting into trouble and would not take discipline. The problems seemed only to worsen when her younger brother was born. Since becoming a teenager, Annette had been arrested on a number of occasions for minor offenses, including shoplifting, curfew violations, and, most recently, underage drinking. When we met Annette, she had just been expelled from school for consuming alcohol at school. The odds were that Annette would be permanently expelled and placed in a special school if her behavior didn't change. After hearing the family's reasons for coming for therapy, we asked if there had been any pretreatment change.

THERAPIST: Well, let me ask you all a question.
[*Family (nods affirmatively.*]
TH: When did you make the appointment to come here?
MOTHER: Let's see. It would have been last Wednesday.
TH: Okay, so nearly a week ago?
MOTHER: Yes.
TH: Since making the appointment to come here last
    Wednesday, what have you noticed that's been better?
[*Family looks at one another.*]
DAD: Well, there haven't been any fights. My wife hasn't
    called me at work. I haven't had to come home from work
    to help get Annette under control.
TH: Hmm. So there haven't been any fights?
DAD: No. In fact [*looking at wife*], I haven't heard my wife
    complain about Annette in the last few days.
[*Annette begins to smile broadly.*]
TH (*looking at wife*): Is that right?
MOTHER: Yes, it is. We've mostly been talking about what to
    do with her [*pointing to Annette*], but I haven't noticed,
    well, she hasn't been . . . she has been, now that I think of
    it, acting *different* these last few days. I'm just waiting for
    the volcano to blow.

❑

The brief excerpt shows how the family was able to identify
some changes in Annette's behavior *that had started before formal treatment was initiated.* As indicated previously, pretreatment change is a frequent and important clue for solving the
problems that bring clients in for treatment. Noticing pretreatment change is, however, only the first step toward using Clue 3
to solve problems. If we stopped at this point in the interview, it
would not be long before, as Annette's mother put it, "the vol-
cano would blow!"

Identifying Your Pretreatment Change Pattern

As was the case with the two previous clues, it is necessary to gather information about the cause of the pretreatment change so that you will be able to repeat it deliberately in the future. Once again, we return to the what, where, who, when, and how questions. Before reading any further, take some time to analyze your experiences of pretreatment change, using the following questions:

- **What . . .**
  . . . did you notice yourself doing differently when you experienced the change?
  . . . did others see you doing when you experienced the change? What exactly did they see you doing that told them you had experienced a change?
  . . . was happening shortly before and after you experienced the change? What else? How did this influence the occurrence of pretreatment change?
  . . . (would/do) others say was happening shortly before and after you experienced the change? What else? How did this influence the occurrence of pretreatment change?
  . . . did you do to bring about this change?
  . . . weren't you doing at the time you experienced the pretreatment change that might have caused the change to happen? What were you doing instead? How did this influence the occurrence of pretreatment change?
  . . . would (you/others) have to see you doing again to convince them that this change was real, not a fluke?
- **Where . . .**
  . . . were you when this change came about? How did this influence the occurrence of pretreatment change?
  . . . were you shortly before or after the change came about that might have influenced its occurrence?
  . . . hadn't you been either before, after or during this change that might have played a role in its occurrence? Where were you instead?

- **Who ...**
  ... was around when you experienced the pretreatment change? How did this influence its occurrence?
  ... was not around when you experienced the pretreatment change? How did this influence its occurrence?
- **When ...**
  ... did you experience the pretreatment change? What role did this play in its occurrence?
- **How ...**
  ... did you make the change come about? What specifically did you do differently that caused the change to happen?
  ... did others help bring about this change? What specifically did they do that influenced the occurrence of the change?

❑

BEATING THE ODDS

To illustrate how these questions can be used to establish the pattern surrounding pretreatment change, let's return to the session with Annette and her parents. This excerpt begins with the therapist asking Annette about the changes her parents are reporting:

THERAPIST *(looking at Annette)*: Is this right what your parents are saying here that things have been better over the last few days?
[*Annette nods affirmatively.*]
TH: *What's* going on?
ANNETTE: I've just not been—I've just been trying to get along better.
TH: You have? *What* have you been doing to get along better?

ANNETTE: I don't want to have to go to that other school.

TH: Uh-huh. So *what* have you been doing to increase your chances that you won't have to go to that other school?

ANNETTE: Trying to get along better.

TH: Uh-huh. And *what* kinds of things have you been doing to get along better?

ANNETTE: Not fighting with my mom or my brother.

TH: *What* have you been doing instead?

ANNETTE *(pauses, looks at mother, laughs):* Biting my tongue.

MOTHER *(smiling):* I've noticed that.

TH: You have? *How* could you tell that Annette was biting her tongue?

MOTHER: Well, she'd start to say something, you know, some smart remark, and then she'd catch herself.

TH *(to Annette):* Is your mom right, Annette? You would start to say something but catch yourself and stop? [*Annette nods affirmatively*].

TH: *How* did you do that?

❑

The therapist continued to explore the pattern and sequence of events surrounding the pretreatment change for several more minutes. The exploration eventually resulted in a clear picture of the events leading up to and following the pretreatment change that Annette and her family had experienced. Included in this pattern were several things that Annette's parents had done but not recognized prior to their being asked the questions. Recognizing the pattern helped the family repeat the changes later and ultimately resulted in Annette's being able to stay in her original school.

GETTING FROM OZ TO KANSAS DEPENDS ON . . . YOU!

If you have read through this chapter but decided not take the time to apply each clue carefully and thoughtfully to your situation, you may want to rethink your decision. If you really want to solve your problem—if you really want to get back to Kansas, so to speak—it will take more than simply reading through this book. In order to be successful, you must actually apply the ideas and techniques that are presented. Few people change only by reading. In this regard there is a great deal of wisdom in the old joke about how many therapists it takes to change a light bulb. The punch line, you may remember, is that changing the light bulb requires only one therapist *but the light bulb has to want to change.*

Many years of research and clinical experience have shown us that the information and strategies contained in this chapter can help problem drinkers construct their own personalized programs for recovery and then use those programs eventually to conquer their problems with alcohol. The benefits that you experience from the methods described in this book will be directly proportional to the amount of time you spend applying them to your specific situation. There simply is no escaping the fact that *you must do the work.*

THE MIRACLE METHOD
READY REFERENCE
❏
THREE CLUES FOR FINDING SOLUTIONS

1. Look for pieces of your miracle that are happening now.
2. Learn from your lack of mistakes.
3. Look for pretreatment change.

5

Making Your Dream a Reality

GETTING ALL YOUR KEYS AND CLUES TO ADD UP TO SOLUTION

First the dream, *then* the reality.
—Robert Alexander
Living Stage Theater Company

The best way to predict the future, is to create it.
—Peter Drucker

Just do it!
—Nike commercial

Like many American boys, Scott developed an avid interest in the art of prestidigitation—magic—as he was growing up. Whenever a famous magician appeared on television, Scott almost certainly could be found in front of the set, carefully scrutinizing the seemingly miraculous feats of magic in order to ascertain how they were accomplished. Initially his parents humored him by purchasing a few magic sets from the local toy store and by taking him to the library to check out books on the subject of magic. Before long, however, Scott had read and studied all the books available at the public library and had outgrown the tricks

❏ 93

contained in the "kiddie" collections that his parents had bought for him. What was worse, however, was that none of the books or kits contained any secrets to the big stage illusions that fascinated Scott the most. A chance event, however, changed all this.

A well-known magician came to a city near Scott's hometown for a performance. Scott was in the audience for that show and, as luck would have it, was chosen to act as the magician's assistant for a few of the illusions that the magician performed. Much to his consternation, however, the various magic effects seemed just as miraculous from his vantage point on the stage as they had from the audience.

Then another piece of good fortune came Scott's way. Following the show the magician informed Scott and his parents that he had been looking for a young assistant to help out with his act. He had enjoyed working with Scott and wondered if he would be interested in the job. "Need you ask?" the expressions on his parents' faces must have communicated. Scott became the magician's assistant. Over the next few years following that chance meeting, Scott apprenticed with the magician, both studying his methods and assisting at his performances.[1]

Let's skip to the end of the story. Scott did learn the secrets behind the majority of illusions performed by magicians. Believe it or not, there were only a few simple secrets and principles. Moreover, much to his surprise, Scott found that *the two most important secrets of magic were practice and hard work.* Hours and hours had to be spent not in learning the secrets of the tricks but in perfecting their delivery at performances.

In the end, as you may already have guessed, Scott did not become a professional magician. Knowing that the two biggest secrets were practice and hard work eventually made magic lose some of its, well, magic. Even so, Scott's experience with the magician taught him something valuable for his work as a psychologist. The same principles apply to the process of trying to change your life for the better. There is an ever-increasing number of treatment programs, books, manuals, and gurus offering ways to help people solve their problems or improve their lives—this book not excepted. Just like the illusions that initially fascinated Scott, the results these various people and products achieve seem magical, even miraculous. On closer inspection, however, they all boil down to two things: practice and hard work.

In the preceding chapters we introduced you to a new way of thinking about change. You mapped out the direction you wanted to go as you answered the "miracle" question and then explored those periods in your life when you experienced the miracle either in part or in whole. In this chapter we will teach you how to convert your miracle into reality by adding all the ideas, keys, and clues together in a way that equals the solution you desire. Thereafter we will show you how to ensure that your solution continues to be a reality. Along the way don't be surprised if some of the magic you were hoping for gives way to the reality of how the miracle of change actually occurs. Don't give up, though, because change requires . . . well, you know.

THE SOLUTION EQUATIONS

The process of making your miracle into a reality starts with converting the ideas, keys, and clues you have learned from your reading up to this point into what we call the solution equations. Basically these equations help you combine the information you have learned thus far in a way that adds up to the solution you desire. Now, we know that by discussing these ideas in terms of mathematics, we run the risk of losing some of you. We urge you, however, not to be frightened by the math. Our equations are based on the simplest of mathematical operations—addition and subtraction only. You don't have to be a genius to figure them out.

With that said, let's take a closer look at the equations. There are three basic solution equations that reflect three basic ways that people use the ideas, keys, and clues of solution-focused thinking to solve their drinking problem. These equations are:

1. M(iracle) + E(xceptions) + x = Solution
2. M(iracle) + E(xceptions) + y = Solution
3. M(iracle) – E(xceptions) + z = Solution

As you can see, each equation contains three variables. You have already learned about and completed the first two variables in each equation since if you think about it, all the ideas, keys, and clues covered in the reading thus far can be placed into one of these two categories. For the sake of convenience, we will be using the term *exception* to refer to all the clues presented in the last chapter. You will recall that these clues included (1) times when pieces of the miracle were already happening, (2) exception periods, and (3) pretreatment change.

You have undoubtedly noticed, however, that each equation also contains a missing variable, a variable, in other words, that has not yet been defined. In order to have an equation add up to solution, it is essential to find the value of the missing variable. Believe it or not, it is possible to find that variable and solve the equation by using the two variables in the equation that you already know—that is, your miracle and exception periods. We will show you how to use your miracle and exceptions to find the missing variable by going through each equation step by step, using stories of clients to illustrate the process. As we do so, look for the story and equation that best match your experience. That equation will be the one you use to add all the ideas, keys, and clues together so that they equal your solution.

Equation 1
1. M(iracle) + E(xceptions) + x = Solution

Tony had been a serious problem drinker for as long as he could remember. By the time he entered treatment with us, he had been through a number of treatment programs and had even spent time in jail because of his alcohol use. Tony finally decided that it was time to do something about his problem when his wife of eleven years, Stephanie, walked out of his life, taking their three-year-old daughter with her. In response to the miracle question, Tony described in detail how he wanted his life to be.

> TONY *(tearful):* I just want another chance to show them how much I love them.
> THERAPIST: And so, after this miracle, Tony, what would you do to show Stephanie and your daughter how much you love them?
> TONY: I would support them, you know, financially, by getting a job and then keeping it.
> TH: Uh-huh. What else?
> TONY: I would do things for Stephanie, too, you know, because she's been the one who has been working.
> TH: What kinds of things would you do for her?
> TONY: I would do things like, cooking dinner, cleaning the house, taking better care of Remy [*daughter*]. Things she has always wanted me to do since I was home.
> TH: Would she notice if you did those things?
> TONY: Oh, yeah, she would notice. She used to tell me all the time, but I didn't pay any attention to it. I just said, you know, "yeah, yeah, yeah" and then did what I wanted. [*tearful.*] Now she's left me.

Tony and the therapist continued to talk about how his life would be different after the miracle. In addition to the changes already mentioned, he talked about spending more "quality time" with his daughter, developing new friends, and, most important, giving up alcohol.

As we explored each of these areas in detail, Tony spontaneously reported that he had not used any alcohol for the eight days before the treatment session. Knowing that such pretreatment change might prove valuable in the search for solutions to Tony's problem, we took the opportunity to explore how he had managed to stay away from alcohol during that period.

After some initial difficulty Tony was able to spell out what he had done in order to be successful. This included, for example, driving a way home from work that did not take him by his usual drinking haunts, not taking calls from his drinking buddies, spending time completing unfinished projects around the house, spending some of his free time in the public library reading books about art and other subjects of personal interest, and, finally, making out what he called his goal sheet for what he wanted to accomplish in the future. When asked, Tony was even able to describe how he had managed to overcome several episodes during the week when he had been sorely tempted to drink.

Tony's story is a perfect example of how the first equation can be used to find the missing variable x so that all the components of change add up to the solution. Let's solve Tony's equation together. The first variable in the equation is the miracle. During the session Tony supplied this variable by answering the miracle question. The second variable is exceptions. Recall that for the sake of space, we will use the term *exception* to refer to all three clues in the preceding chapter (that is, exceptions, instances or times when pieces of the miracle are happening, and pretreatment change). Tony provided this second variable by identifying an eight-day period of pretreatment change during which he was experiencing some parts of what he wanted. In addition, he was able to describe the *deliberate actions* he had taken to cause the exceptions to occur. Remember the concrete steps Tony had taken in order to be successful?

Believe it or not, this is all the information we need in order to solve the equation for the missing variable x. Think about it for a minute. If you (1) know what you want and (2) are able to describe periods of time when that has happened and (3) know what you did or are doing in order to make that happen, the only thing that remains to get the equation to add up to solution is simply to do more of it! The complete equation, therefore, is:

$$M\text{(iracle)}$$
$$E\text{(xceptions)}$$
$$+ Do \text{ (more of what works)}$$
$$= \text{S O L U T I O N}$$

As you can see, *your* doing more of what works is the missing variable in this first solution equation. It is also precisely what we told Tony to do at the conclusion of the first session of treatment.

Tony returned the following week and reported that he had continued to do what had worked for him the first eight days. Reflecting on that strategy later during the session, he said, "I've been busy keeping the things I want in my head and then going at it instead of just sitting around the house and moping and thinking." Then with great insight he added, *"Because, if I think and do, then I think it will come back on me . . .* you know, just like if I think and do drink, then that comes back on me, too."

Tony came for a total of six visits, each time reporting how he was continuing to think about and do what he knew worked for him. He further noticed that the changes he experienced as a result of doing more of what works began to snowball into other areas of his life. As this book is being written, Tony is enrolled in a local technical college and is back together with his wife and daughter.

Equation 2

$M\text{(iracle)} + E\text{(xceptions)} + y = \text{Solution}$

Martin was told by his employer that he had to seek treatment or would lose his job. When we asked him, Martin freely admitted drinking but denied having a serious alcohol problem. Every once in a while, he told us, his drinking simply "got out of control." He then ended up being late for work, calling in sick, or missing work entirely. His personal life, he added, also suffered when his control over alcohol somehow managed to slip between his fingers.

When asked the miracle question, Martin answered that his employer would stop worrying about him and that he would be able to keep his job. He liked what he did for a living and was aware that keeping his job would require an improvement in his performance at work. Doing better, he further understood, would require that he somehow manage to stay sober. We quickly began to explore those periods when pieces of the miracle that Martin had described were already happening in his life as well as times when he somehow managed to stay sober.

Not surprisingly there were many examples of each. However, in contrast with Tony, Martin could not spell out with any degree of specificity how he managed to experience success on those occasions. For him, the pieces of the miracle and exception periods just seemed to happen randomly, to be beyond his control. When he was pressed to explain what was different about those days he did not use alcohol to the point of difficulty, the most he could come up with as an answer was that he "just didn't feel like it" or that he "woke up on the right side of the bed" or something equally vague. Martin could see no rhyme or reason, no pattern, in other words, in his occasional successes.

THERAPIST: Martin, what is different about those times when you don't drink?

MARTIN: I'm not sure.

TH: How do you explain that sometimes you are able to be successful in controlling your drinking?

MARTIN (*thinking*): Hmm. I really don't know. Sometimes it just seems like I don't want any. You know, I get up and go to work. The thought just doesn't cross my mind.

TH: And you can go for how long like that?

MARTIN: Well, days, weeks. Sometimes, in the past, I've gone for months without it [alcohol] entering my mind.

TH: How do you do that?

MARTIN: I wish I knew that. To me, it just seems as if the thought doesn't enter my mind.

TH: Anything you do different during those times that you think might contribute to your being successful?

MARTIN: Truthfully, it just seems to happen.

The interview continued in much the same fashion for a while longer. Martin simply could not identify what was different about the periods when he was successful. Indeed, at one point he said that he could not predict when the successes would happen since they seemed to occur as randomly as the "flip of a coin."

What can one do in such instances? Clearly it would be ludicrous to suggest that Martin do more of what works since he could not describe the deliberate actions he took to bring about the successful periods. So what could Martin do to get his equation to add up to solution? What is the missing variable in equations where exceptions occur randomly rather than deliberately?

Believe it or not, we once again have enough information to solve the equation for the missing variable. Let's solve the equation together, starting with the variables we know for sure. The first variable in the equation is the miracle. During the session Martin supplied this variable by answering the "miracle" question. The second variable in the equation is exceptions; Martin provided this variable by identifying and then describing those times when he had experienced some parts of what he wanted. Remember, however, that Martin was not able to describe the deliberate actions he had taken in order to cause the exceptions to occur. Rather, the exceptions seem to occur randomly.

Take a moment to think about the equation. If you (1) know what you want and (2) are able to describe periods of time when what you want has happened but (3) those times seem to occur randomly, then the only thing that remains to get the equation to equal solution is to do something that causes the successful periods to occur less randomly—to occur, in other words, more deliberately. What might that be? Well, Martin actually hinted at two ideas that our clients find help exceptions occur more deliberately. To these two, we add a third idea.

Predicting the Future

The first idea is to try to predict either when or whether an exception period will occur. The most productive way to do this is to make a prediction every night before you go to bed about what kind of day the next day will be. Will it be, in other words, more like a miracle day, a day in which you experience what you want either in whole or in part? Or, on the other hand, will it be just a normal day, kind of business as usual? Write the prediction you make on a piece of paper, and store it in a safe place.

The following night take out the paper containing your prediction, and see whether you were right or wrong. Most important, make an accounting to yourself about why you were either right or wrong. The more specific you are, the more information you will obtain. The more information you obtain about the occurrence of exception periods, the more likely you are to learn some deliberate actions you can take in order to cause those periods to happen deliberately in the future. In this regard some questions that you might find helpful in analyzing your predictions are:

- What exactly did you do to contribute to the outcome, whatever it was?
- What would others say you did to contribute to the outcome, whatever it was?
- What did others do to contribute to the outcome?

- On the basis of this information, how will your prediction be different tomorrow?
- What is your prediction for tomorrow?

Turning Your Future over to Fate

Let's take a look at the second idea that Martin suggested. Recall that he described his experience of successful periods as random in nature, indeed, like the "flip of a coin." For an as-yet-undetermined reason, some people find that turning control of such occurrences completely over to chance results paradoxically in their having more control over the desired behavior. For this reason we sometimes recommend what we call the coin toss exercise.

The coin toss is simple and can be a particularly useful first step in learning to gain control over randomly occurring exception periods. Basically it involves flipping a coin and then doing some predetermined behavior depending on whether the coin turns up heads or tails. We have found that the task is most helpful when it is completed in the morning before you start your day. You can try the exercise yourself by tossing a coin each morning before you get out of bed. If the coin happens to turn up heads, then it is predetermined that all day long you will *pretend as much and as completely as possible that you are having a miracle day*, a day that, in other words, resembles the picture you painted for yourself in Chapter 3, regardless of how the day actually unfolds and irrespective of what others may think or do during it. In fact, we strongly recommend that you not inform others about what you are doing. Instead, merely notice what is different about them and what you believe they might be noticing different about you as you pretend the miracle is happening.

On the other hand, if the coin turns up tails, then it is predetermined that all day long you just have one of your normal days. Once again keep track of what you notice about others as you pretend to have one of your normal days regardless of how the day develops or what these others may think or do.

The Solution Lottery

One final task that some of our clients find useful in making their random exceptions more deliberate is what we call the solution lottery. This assignment works by bringing powerful principles of behavioral psychology to bear on the occurrence of exception periods. It is also fun. You can put these powerful principles—and fun—to work for you by completing the following three steps. First, make a list of activities and things you enjoy and, most important, find reinforcing. These might include taking a walk, playing a round of golf, talking with a friend on the phone, buying a new book or article of clothing, or sleeping in an extra hour.

The activities on your list should not require a great deal of preparation or cost a lot of money. Any activity can be considered reinforcing *if* you are willing to engage in other less enjoyable or desirable behaviors first in order to have the opportunity to experience the desired activity at some later point. The longer you make the list, the better.

Second, get a small paper sack, such as a lunch bag, or some other small container, such as a small cardboard box, and a sheet of paper. Tear the paper into five strips. On each of the five strips write one of the following phrases: "no reward," "immediate reward," "reward in four hours," "reward in twelve hours," and "reward in twenty-four hours." Third, and last, put the five strips of paper in the paper bag or container and mix them up. Now you're ready to begin the solution lottery.

You start the lottery by making a concerted effort to look out for the occurrence of exceptions. Whenever you happen to notice an exception, be it a piece of the miracle happening or a time when the problem does not happen, you take out your list and pick one of the rewarding activities. Then reach into the paper sack containing the strips of paper, withdraw one of the strips, and follow the directions. For example, if the strip of paper indicates "no reward," then you do not engage in the activity you chose from the list. On the other hand, if the paper instructs you to reward yourself immediately, then you do the desired activity without delay. Similarly, if the paper indicates "reward in twelve hours," you engage in the rewarding activity twelve hours after the exception has occurred.

Please note that whenever the lottery tells you to postpone the reward for a given period, you should give yourself the reward at the designated time regardless of what is going on when the reward is to be given or of what has transpired between the occurrence of the exception and the time the reward is to be given. You may be tempted, for example, not to give yourself a delayed reward if you are engaging in some undesirable activity at the time the reward is supposed to be given. Give yourself the reward anyway. You may also be tempted not to give yourself the delayed reward if you have engaged in some undesirable behavior between the occurrence of the exception and the time the reward should be given. Give yourself the reward anyway. Even if you don't feel as if you deserve the reward, you should give it to yourself.

One final comment on the solution lottery. If you find yourself in a situation where administering the reward at the appointed hour is inconvenient, impossible, or likely to make matters worse (e.g., leaving work, getting up in the middle of the night), then you have a choice. Either you can review your list of rewarding activities and choose something that you can do at the appointed hour or you can reward yourself at the first available moment. The purpose of the lottery is to interrupt habitual patterns of behavior so that new patterns can emerge, *not* to exacerbate your problems. So be reasonable. If for some reason it is not possible to give yourself the reward at the appointed hour, choose something else or give yourself the reward later.

In summary; the idea behind all three of these suggestions is the same: Do something to make random occurrences of the miracle, exceptions, or pretreatment change more deliberate. That's all. Simple. The complete second equation reads:

M(iracle)
E(xceptions)
+ Do (something that makes random
    exceptions more deliberate)
_____
= S O L U T I O N

By the way, remember Martin? Well, at the conclusion of his first session with us we suggested that he try the coin toss. Much to our surprise, he returned for his second visit reporting that he had experienced "a very discouraging week." Defying all the laws of probability, Martin had somehow managed to flip tails *every day* following his first session. Being forced to have a normal day had, however, made Martin notice how he actually did contribute to the occurrence of problem periods in his life. In the sessions that followed, Martin's luck changed, and he experienced a more even distribution of heads and tails. Over time he gradually learned how to create the exception periods both more deliberately and more regularly. In addition, he discovered that these periods were noticed by others, in particular his employer, and rewarded appropriately. At last contact Martin continues to work for his same employer.

Equation 3

3. M(iracle) − E(xceptions) + z = Solution

By any standard, Michelle grew up in a "dysfunctional family." Both her parents had been problem drinkers. Her father drank nearly every day, Michelle recalled, and when drunk, he was often verbally and physically abusive toward his wife and young children. Michelle's mother, on the other hand, attempted to conceal her use of alcohol from the family. Unlike her husband, she spent most days locked in the bedroom, withdrawn, depressed, and unresponsive to Michelle and her siblings.

Like both her siblings, Michele eventually began to develop a drinking problem of her own. Initially she drank to cover up the feelings of sadness and depression she had about her family and home life. Later she discovered that alcohol had other benefits for her. For example, drinking seemed to help her overcome some strong feelings of shyness and inadequacy that she experienced, especially in relationships with men. Even a small amount, she told us, helped her feel less inhibited and more capable of interacting with others. She recognized, however, that her drinking also had a downside. For example, she had taken some risks while drinking that she never would have taken when sober, such as having unprotected sex with a stranger. More important, she recognized that while her drinking may have helped start most of her relationships, it was also usually responsible for ending them.

Drinking was not the only problem that Michelle was struggling with. Prior to coming to see us, she had seen another counselor who told her that she had an eating disorder. She told us that she also felt unresolved about her past, in particular, her relationships with her mother and father as well as with her two siblings, with whom she had lost contact over the last few years. Both, she told us, had been struggling with alcohol the last time she saw them.

"There are so many problems to be dealt with," she said at one point in the session, "that I don't know where to start." We saw our opportunity and asked Michelle to imagine that a miracle had taken place and the problems that brought her to our office were solved. She responded by telling us that she had frequently imagined and fantasized about just such an occurrence as she was growing up. For this reason, perhaps, Michelle was able to answer the miracle question in considerable detail.

THERAPIST: Michelle, let me ask you a strange kind of question.

MICHELLE: Okay.

TH: It takes some pretending on your part. Here is how it goes. Suppose tonight, you go home, go to bed, and fall asleep. And while you are sleeping, a miracle happens, and the miracle is that these problems that brought you here today are solved. Just like that! But because you were asleep, you didn't know that this miracle had happened. When you woke up the next morning, what would be some of the first things that you would notice that would tell you that a miracle had happened?

MICHELLE: It's funny that you should ask me that question.

TH: Hmm. Why's that?

MICHELLE: Well, because I had this really, *really* bad childhood, I used to spend a lot of time alone in my room wishing a miracle would happen. It never did.

TH: Hmm. Suppose one did happen now, Michelle. Suppose you finally got your wish and the miracle did happen now. What would be different in your life tomorrow that would tell you that the miracle had happened?

MICHELLE: Well, I guess the first thing that I would notice if the miracle happened would be that my appearance would change.

TH: Okay.

MICHELLE: I would be taking care of myself. I would start wearing nice clothes again. Dressing up. Doing my hair and my nails. Eating right.

TH: Uh-huh.

MICHELLE: Right now I just eat whatever I feel like, and so after the miracle I would be watching what I eat. I wouldn't be going to all the fast-food restaurants and pigging out all the time.

TH: So you would be taking better care of yourself?

MICHELLE: Uh-huh, and that would make me feel better about myself. Because right now I have a really, *really* low self-esteem.

TH: No wonder.

MICHELLE: Right. And I would be more of a positive person. Put it this way: I wouldn't doubt myself so much. I would just go in there and do whatever I had to do whether in my job or with my family.

TH: What else?

MICHELLE: I wouldn't let others walk over me anymore.

TH: What would you do instead?

MICHELLE: I would just tell them they couldn't do that to me. Not in any mean way or anything, but I just wouldn't let people take advantage of me anymore.

TH: Uh-huh.

MICHELLE: I guess more of the real me would come out.

TH: Tell me more about that. How would you know that more of the real you was coming out?

MICHELLE: I'm a really friendly person. Nobody knows it, though.

TH: And so after the miracle?

MICHELLE: I would be getting out and meeting people, talking with people at work, you know, going out sometimes.

Michelle continued to describe her miracle for several minutes. Her description eventually included statements about how her use of alcohol would be different after the miracle. For Michelle, her miracle was that she would be completely abstinent from alcohol. She believed that the memories of her parents' drinking and the problems that alcohol had caused in her own life left her no other choice. Using Key 4, we helped Michelle specify what she would be doing instead of drinking.

When we finally got around to asking her about times when pieces of her miracle had already happened, however, she had no answer. For her there simply were no times when pieces of the miracle had happened in her life. Further, she could not recall any times when the issues that had brought her to treatment were not problems for her, with the exception of her childhood and early adolescence. These times, we agreed, were too remote to be of any value in finding solutions to her problems. When we asked Michelle if she had noticed any changes in her life for the better since making the appointment to come in for treatment, she shook her head slowly from left to right. Then, with her head bowed, she confessed that she had actually taken a few drinks from a flask she kept in her car just before coming into our office.

Unfortunately Michelle's story was not new to us. Indeed, we had heard similar stories many times before. The good news, of course, was that Michelle was getting help. Perhaps because more information is available about the negative effects of problem drinking on children and families, more people like Michelle are seeking treatment services. Frequently, however, people raised in these environments cannot recall times when the problems that they are hoping to change have not been present in their life—even momentarily. There simply aren't any pieces of the miracle. There are no exceptions. There is no pretreatment change. In short, the person has no firsthand experience—or, at least, cannot recall any firsthand experience at that moment—of the outcome he or she desires.

So what can you do in such instances if, for example, you know what you want but do not have or cannot recall any firsthand experience of having what you want, from pieces of the miracle happening, from exceptions in the past, or from pretreatment change? What can you do in order to get the equation to equal a solution? Well, let's think about it once again. Two things are certain: (1) You know what you want, and (2) you have not experienced it before. What remains? Well, going out and somehow getting the experience, of course!

Now how, you may ask, can you just go out and get this experience that we are talking about? The answer: *by pretending.* In other words, the missing variable in the third and last solution equation is your acting as if the miracle that you are looking for has already happened or is just beginning to unfold in your life. We often tell clients, for example, to pick a few days in the week following their first session to pretend that the miracle has happened and to notice what is different about both themselves and others. Therefore, the third and last solution equation is:

$$
\frac{
\begin{array}{l}
M(\text{iracle}) \\
E(\text{xceptions}) \\
+ \textit{Act as If} \text{ (the miracle has happened)}
\end{array}
}{}
$$

$$= S \; O \; L \; U \; T \; I \; O \; N$$

In fact, acting as if the miracle had happened is precisely what we asked Michelle to do at the conclusion of her first session of treatment.

Not convinced? Well, as a way of illustrating the value of acting *as if,* let's look at the way many of us pretend in our everyday lives. Take a moment to think back to the very first day you were on your job. Fresh out of school, perhaps, but with no experience. Right? Well, what did you do? Ask to go back to school for more education? Ask for less responsibility? Tell your supervisor and coworkers that you didn't really know what you were doing and that they should lower their expectations accordingly? Probably not. If you are like most people, you didn't do any of these things. Rather, you pretended you knew exactly what you were doing from the moment you interviewed for the position through your first few days and weeks on the job. Over time your pretending gradually turned into real-life experience, knowledge, and skills.

Alcoholics Anonymous has an expression for this idea: Fake it until you make it! People usually think they need to get more information before they can start changing their lives for the better. They look to experts, attend a workshop or seminar, or read the latest self-help book. There is nothing inherently wrong with any of these strategies. In the end, however, you still have to go out and try it. In other words, in the end, you still have to act as if you know what you are doing. So in reality you don't need to learn more about what to do. Rather, you need to do more of what you want to do.

In Michelle's case, she actually laughed when we told her the assignment. "I can already think of some things," she told us, "that I'm going to do." Much to our surprise, when she returned the following week, she told us that she had contacted her siblings and informed them that she was not going to let their parents ruin her life any longer. They had, she told them, stolen her childhood, and she was not going to allow their problems to affect her future. In short, she was straightening out her life. If her siblings needed any help, she told them, they could lean on her. "Was this just pretending on your part?" we asked. She hesitated momentarily and then responded, "I really didn't think about it as pretending at that moment. No, definitely not pretending. I meant it."

She then informed us that the two days she had picked to pretend that the miracle had taken place were the first two days she had not had a drink for as far back as she could remember. The difference showed on her face. Her eyes were clear, and she wore a broad smile. Her experience now empowered her and formed the foundation for change in other problem areas of her life.

Could It Be This Simple?

That's exactly what one of our clients asked us not too long ago. The man, a chronic problem drinker who was also a diagnosed schizophrenic, claimed that he had finally had enough and wanted to change his life. He was in his mid-forties and had had many previous treatments for both alcohol and mental health problems. He told us, for example, that he had been in a number of inpatient alcoholism treatment programs, had been given a number of different medications, and had even spent several months in a residential treatment center. "None of these treatments worked," he said with a sad tone in his voice. "I always end up drinking again. The voices always come back."

The therapist saw the obvious opening to explore those periods when the man had been successful and, seizing the opportunity, asked him to talk about his having been sober and not troubled by the voices and other problems people experience when they are suffering from schizophrenia. For the next hour the client and therapist talked about the many times the man had experienced the kind of life that he now desired. As the session drew to a close, the client suddenly grew silent and contemplative. Then, with a tone of surprise in his voice, he asked the therapist, "Could it be this simple?"

The answer to the client's question was and is, we believe, an unequivocal "Yes!" The solution often is just this simple. Find out what works, and do more of it. As we told you in Chapter 3, however, simple and easy are not the same. The ideas we are presenting are indeed simple. The reality is, however, that hard work and practice are required in order to convert these relatively simple ideas into lasting solutions. Creating a formula for a lasting solution is the topic to which we now turn our attention.

FINDING *YOUR* FORMULA FOR CHANGE

We began this chapter by introducing you to the solution equations. The three equations we presented were designed to help you take the first steps toward converting your miracle into reality. In order to ensure that your miracle continues over time, however, it will be necessary to experiment with the equations until you find your own individual formula for change. This is where the real work starts. We warn you that simply reading the following information will probably not be enough to ensure lasting change. If you haven't already done so, now is the time to put the ideas you have been reading about into practice.

At this point you have all the information you need to begin converting your miracle into reality. We suggest that you start this process by taking the equation (or equations) that best describe your experience and applying it or them to your situation for at least one week. Along the way you can always remind yourself of the various equations by referring to the solution-focused Miracle Method Ready Reference at the conclusion of this chapter. Please feel free to modify the equations as you see fit. As we mentioned earlier, these three equations are the basic, not the only, ways that people combine the various keys, clues, and information presented in the book.

While you are applying the equation or equations to your situation, keep a watchful eye out for any changes that occur. In particular, look out for times when pieces of your miracle happen or when your problem does not happen. You must be diligent in watching for such changes in these early stages. Initial changes are usually small; they frequently go unnoticed or are dismissed as insignificant. This is unfortunate since these changes are often the start of solutions that have the potential for growing and becoming lasting therapeutic change.

Butterflies, Snowballs, and Ripples

The expression *the butterfly effect* was coined by the meteorologist Edward Lorenz to describe his observation of how very small changes in one weather system could result in dramatic changes in other weather systems. Lorenz found, for example, that changes as small and seemingly insignificant as a butterfly flapping its wings in South America could result in changes as large and dramatic as a hurricane occurring in the Gulf of Mexico.[2]

A similar observation of how small changes can lead to larger changes was made with regard to human behavior. Researchers H. Spiegel and L. Linn noted that small changes in behavior frequently initiated a complex series of interactions that eventually resulted in dramatic overall change.[3] They termed their discovery the ripple effect after the phenomenon that is observed when a stone is tossed into a calm body of water. Other experts in the field of human behavior have described change as a "matter of tipping the first domino" or rolling a snowball down a hill.[4]

In each of the case examples presented in this chapter, small changes initiated through the use of the solution equations eventually led to larger changes. Call it the butterfly, ripple, snowball, or domino effect, a small change can have profound and far-reaching consequences. Because such changes are so important, it is useful to take note of any and all of them. One useful way to keep track of the changes, or differences, you are looking for and notice during the week is to create what we call a solution graph.

The Solution Graph

The solution graph contains a horizontal and a vertical axis. You can make your own solution graph using a pencil, ruler, and a blank piece of paper. Some people find graph paper helpful, but it is not necessary. Any blank piece of paper will do.

First, draw the horizontal axis. This is the line running from left to right along the bottom of the paper. Along this axis, write the days of the week, beginning with the day that you will start applying the solution equations. For example, if you will be starting on Monday, the horizontal axis of your solution graph should be:

MON.　　TUES.　　WED.　　THURS.　　FRI.　　SAT.　　SUN.

Next, draw the vertical axis. This is the line running up and down the left side of the paper. Start the vertical axis beginning at the farthest left point of the vertical axis and drawing upward. Along this axis, write the numbers 1 to 10. For example:

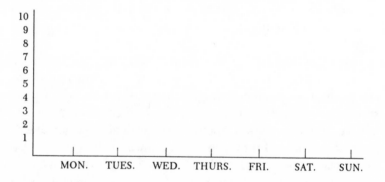

Voilà! You have completed your very own solution graph, which can now be used to keep track of your observations of change during the week.

Here is how you use the graph. At the conclusion of each day ask yourself the following question: On a scale from 1 to 10, where 10 is that the miracle has happened and 1 is the worst things have ever been, where is today on the scale? After deciding where your day falls on the scale from 1 to 10, the next step is to chart that rating on the graph. To do this, you simply find that point on the graph where the day you are rating intersects with the number you have given that day. For example, if you rated your first day of applying the solution equation a 3, then you would plot a point on the graph at that number above the first day on your chart:

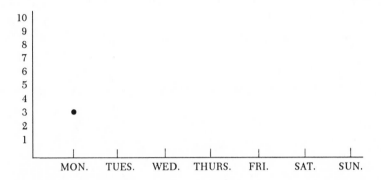

Your work is not finished, however. It is not enough simply to plot the day on the graph. You must also take some time to reflect on the characteristics of the day that resulted in your rating. As you reflect, you may find the following questions helpful in organizing your thoughts about the day. Please feel free to modify your rating once you have considered these questions:

- What was better today? Even just a little? What else?
- What would others (your spouse, employer, children, friends) say was better? Even just a little?
- How was today better?
- What did you do to contribute to today's rating?
- What didn't you do that may have contributed to today's rating?
- What would others (your spouse, employer, children, friends) say you did or did not do that may have contributed to today's rating?
- What have you learned today that you need to do more of in the future? Less of in the future?

As the week progresses, continue to rate and plot each day. Don't be lulled into not completing the graph if every day seems to be going well. *It is not enough to have good days.* It is imperative that you know how those good days come about so that you can continue to have them in the future and so that you can know what to do to when things are not going well. For this reason, take time each day to rate and reflect. In the early stages you may find it helpful to write down your reflections.

❑

MOVING ON UP

As an example, consider Dennis. Dennis was a junior member of a high-profile accounting firm who began drinking to cope with the stress at work. At his first session of treatment he responded to the miracle question by saying that he would find other methods for dealing with the stress at work, begin spending time again with his wife and their new baby, and develop some friends and activities that were not work-related. When he returned for his second session of treatment, the therapist started the session by asking Dennis about what had been better since the initial visit.

> THERAPIST: So, Dennis, *what's* been better since last time?
> DENNIS: Well, I'd say things have been a lot better this last week.
> TH: That's great.
> DENNIS: Yeah, it feels a lot better.
> TH: Let me ask you then, on a scale of one to ten, where ten is the best things could be and one is when things were at their worst, where would you say things were today?
> DENNIS: I'd say a four.
> TH: A four?

DENNIS: Yeah, about a four.

TH: And let's see here, the last time you were here you said things were . . .

DENNIS: A one.

TH: A one, the worst.

DENNIS: Yeah.

TH: So it sounds as if things have been improving.

DENNIS: Slowly but surely. Things seem to be "moving on up," like the song says.

TH: Great! So, help me understand this, *what* exactly has been better?

DENNIS: Well, I've been trying to come home a little earlier from work instead of staying there until all hours of the night.

TH: Hmm.

DENNIS: My wife, when we were first married, used to cook dinner most nights. When I started working at my current job and staying late, she stopped.

TH: Uh-huh. And so did she notice when you came home earlier?

DENNIS: Oh, yeah, she was kind of shocked when I walked in that first night. She wasn't expecting me. I didn't call to tell her that I was coming home at a normal hour, so she was real surprised.

TH: Uh-huh. *What* difference did that make?

DENNIS: It didn't—not that night at least. Things were still pretty strained.

TH: When did you first notice that coming home a little earlier was making a difference between you and Susan?

DENNIS: Probably not until Saturday. I usually go in to work for a few hours on the weekend, and I think she was expecting that I'd just do the usual thing—go into work, that is—but I didn't.

TH: You didn't?

DENNIS: Nope.

TH: *How* did you do that?

❑

In the dialogue that followed, Dennis identified how the changes had come about and exactly what differences these changes had made in his relationship with Susan. Not surprisingly perhaps, Susan and Dennis were intimate on that Saturday evening for the first time in a long while. Identifying the differences, as well as the pattern of events that may have caused them, is essential to being able to repeat them in the future.

As the days accumulate, additional information can be obtained by comparing your ratings across several days. In particular, reflect on the difference between the days that are higher on the scale and those that are lower on the scale. For example, say that the first four days of your graph look like this:

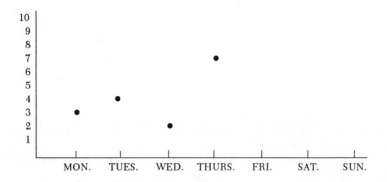

From the graph it is easy to determine that the two best days of the week were Tuesday, which rated a 4, and Thursday, which rated a 7. Additional information can be obtained by reflecting on what was different about those two days that made them better than either Monday, which rated a 3, and Thursday, which rated only a 2. The more specific you are in your descriptions of these differences, the better. One way to do this is to use the who, what, when, where, and how format described in the last chapter. For example:

- **What . . .**
  . . . days were higher on the scale?
  . . . was different about the days that were better?
  . . . did you do before, after, or during the days that may have contributed to their being better?
  . . . didn't you do before, after, or during the days that may have contributed to their being better?
  . . . did you do differently from the days that did not go as well?
- **Who . . .**
  . . . was around when the days were better?
  . . . wasn't around when the days were better?
- **Where . . .**
  . . . were you when the better days happened? How was this different from the days that were not as good?
  . . . hadn't you been before, after, or while these better days were happening? How was this different from the days that did not go as well?
- **When . . .**
  . . . did you notice that these days were better? What role did the time of day, day of the week, week of the month play in these days' being better? How was this different from the days that did not go as well?
- **How . . .**
  . . . could you make these better days happen again?
  . . . could others help to make these better days happen again?

WARNING: We know that it is tempting to spend time reflecting on the days that did not live up to your hopes and expectations. Indeed, as we have already pointed out, most traditional treatment is given over to analyzing and reflecting on such failures. As we hope we have made abundantly clear, however, we have found that such reflections are not particularly useful in helping clients find a formula for change that works for them. Focus instead on what is different about the days when you are successful.

Finding the right formula for change is a process of trial and error, a process for which there is unfortunately no shortcut. By your creating a solution graph and reflecting on your daily experience of this process, however, we hope to help you navigate through the process as quickly and painlessly as possible. Along the way it is almost certain that you will encounter some obstacles. Moreover, you will probably experience some slips and setbacks. The next chapter explores what to do when this happens.

THE MIRACLE METHOD
READY REFERENCE
❑

THE SOLUTION EQUATIONS

Equation 1:

M(iracle)
E(xceptions)
$+ Do$ (more of what works)

$= S O L U T I O N$

Equation 2:

M(iracle)
E(xceptions)
$+ Do$ (something that makes random
     exceptions more deliberate)

$= S O L U T I O N$

Equation 3:

M(iracle)
E(xceptions)
$+ Act\ as\ If$ (the miracle has happened)

$= S O L U T I O N$

FINDING *YOUR* FORMULA FOR CHANGE

1. Look for times when pieces of your miracle are happening.
2. Look for times when your problem is not happening.
3. Be on the lookout for small changes rather than big changes.
4. Complete the solution graph daily.
5. Identify the who, what, when, where, and how of any change.

6

Help! I've Fallen and I Can't Get Up!

THREE RULES FOR DEALING WITH SETBACKS ALONG THE PATH TO SOLUTION

> You always pass failure on the way to success.
> —Mickey Rooney

> Only those who dare to fail greatly can ever achieve greatly.
> —Robert F. Kennedy

> Just keep going. Everybody gets better if they keep at it.
> —Ted Williams

In these modern times nearly everyone has had the experience of being stuck in bumper-to-bumper traffic on the highway. You inch along for a half hour or so, changing the radio from one station to the next, all the while wondering what might be causing the jam-up. A traffic accident? Congested off-ramps? Too many cars merging into traffic from an on-ramp? Suddenly the traffic clears. As you pass the original point of congestion, you notice that there hasn't been any accident and that the on- and off-ramps are all flowing smoothly. In short, you cannot find any good reason for the traffic mess that you have been sitting in for the last half hour. You speed up, driving by and shaking your head disapprovingly at what you assume are some of the potential offenders.

As you drive on, your mind wanders, and you try to figure out what might have caused the tie-up. Perhaps, you hypothesize, there had been an accident earlier at that point on the expressway and the jam-up was merely a remnant. Perhaps a highway patrol officer had been issuing a ticket and traffic had slowed down to rubberneck. By the time you finally drove by, however, the officer and lawbreaking motorist had already finished their business and left. Perhaps, perhaps, perhaps. The truth is, however, there doesn't seem to be any reasonable explanation for the jam.

So what does cause these traffic jams and what exactly causes them to clear up just as quickly and inexplicably? Well, there is, in fact, an answer.[1] People who study these sorts of things term the phenomenon the "shock wave effect" and point out that such jams result from people driving *too cautiously*. Now, you may be thinking, is there such a thing as being too cautious when it comes to something as potentially dangerous as driving? The answer is yes.

Experts point out that most people drive best when traveling at speeds of thirty-five miles per hour or more. Traffic jams are born, they say, when a few motorists begin driving below these optimum speeds—usually in response to increased volume on the expressways—forcing other drivers to react by slowing down. These drivers in turn begin searching for the reason they had to slow down in the first place. The more they search, the more slowly and cautiously they drive. The more slowly and cautiously they drive, the more fearful they become. The more fearful they become, the more they overreact to even the most minor of traffic events, and *voilà!* the traffic jam is born and, most important, for no apparent reason.

Interestingly we have observed a similar shock wave effect

among problem drinkers who experience setbacks along the way to solution. Moreover, we have found that the phenomenon seems to affect treatment professionals as much as the problem drinkers themselves—often more so. How? Well, both are seduced into spending valuable time analyzing and dissecting the setbacks in the hope of finding a reason for them, assuming that knowing the reason will lead to fewer problems in the future. Of course, in order to analyze the setbacks, the process of change has to be slowed down. Slowing down, however, causes the treatment professional and the problem drinker to become more cautious. Becoming more cautious in turn causes both to become more fearful that a setback may occur. Being more fearful leads both to overreact to even the most minor of life events, and *voilà!* the treatment jam is born. Thereafter weeks, months, and even years may be spent in treatment as the professional and the problem drinker attempt to navigate out of the jam that the treatment led to in the first place. Indeed, the consequences of the shock wave effect may be responsible for the widely held belief that overcoming problem drinking is a lifelong process. No wonder! These days nearly everyone has been caught in a traffic jam that seemed to take a lifetime to clear up.

The truth is that setbacks—like traffic jams—are common occurrences along the road to change. This is true, by the way, for *any* problem behavior a person might be trying to change, but it appears doubly so when that behavior is problem drinking. Indeed, research suggests that as many as 90 percent of problem drinkers experience some degree of failure in the first few months of trying to change.[2] Given that setbacks are, therefore, the rule rather the exception, what is the problem drinker supposed to do about them? Well, the first thing is not to panic.

DON'T PANIC!

Panicked drivers, you will recall, are in part responsible for creating the very jam-ups in which they get stuck. We all moan and complain about the other driver or drivers when the truth is that our own behavior—in the form of slowing down, driving overcautiously, rubbernecking, and searching for reasons for a jam—creates and maintains the problem. The experience—and solution—are not unlike that old party favor known as Chinese fingercuffs. Remember those ingenious little devices? You insert your index fingers in opposite sides of a hollow straw tube and then try to remove them. The only problem is that when you try to pull your fingers out of the tube, it tightens, thereby trapping your fingers inside. The harder you pull, the tighter the tube becomes. Unless you are still walking around with your fingers stuck in one of these, you soon discover that *the solution is the opposite of what comes naturally*—that is, a panicked pulling of the fingers outward. Rather, the solution is to push your fingers together first and then remove them.

The same is true of traffic jams that experts say clear up—are solved, in other words—when someone or some group of drivers begins driving once again at the optimum speed of thirty-five miles per hour or more. It is then that the phenomenon we have all witnessed occurs: The expressway tie-ups simply disappear. Of course, this is not what comes naturally to most of us. Rather, we all seem compelled to stop, inspect, and attempt to understand, despite the fact that we rarely find a good reason for the tie-up.

The same is true of setbacks along the road to solution. Problem drinkers and professionals alike seem to want to stop, inspect, and understand the setback even though this is generally not the most helpful strategy for getting back on course. This typical behavior is based on the belief that understanding present setbacks will enable us to avoid setbacks in the future. However, in approaching setbacks, we have found that the focus of attention should be not on understanding present and avoiding future setbacks but rather on how to resume driving at optimum speed on the road to solution once a setback has been experienced.

To be fair, we must admit that we have not always held this view. Rather, like most treatment professionals, we originally learned to analyze and dissect the setbacks our clients experienced in the hopes of preventing future mishaps. Then we met Blythe. Although we did not know it at the time, our interaction with this client eventually led us to an entirely new perspective on the subject.

❑

LEARNING FROM THE LIBRARIAN

We had not heard from Blythe in quite some time when she called urgently requesting an appointment. This did not mean, however, that we had forgotten the thirty-five-year-old school librarian. Blythe did not fit the picture of someone you would immediately think of as having a drinking problem. She was an attractive, talented, and well-educated person who was seeking treatment because she desperately wanted a promotion that was being offered in her department. The problem was, however, that the position required random drug screens. Despite having successfully hidden her problem from others during her tenure at the library, Blythe knew that she would not be able to beat this test.

During our original contact we worked with Blythe for a total of four visits over a period of two months. In that time she developed and implemented her own personal plan for solution. A fifth appointment had been scheduled two months following the fourth session, but Blythe did not appear. She did, however, complete and return our standard follow-up questionnaire, which was mailed to her after she had missed the scheduled session. On the form Blythe indicated that she had stopped coming to treatment because she had "successfully met the goals for therapy." Included with the questionnaire was a brief letter thanking us for our help and reporting that she had passed the first job interviews, including the initial drug screen.

As had been the case during her original visits, Blythe was prompt for the emergency appointment. Much to our surprise, however, she immediately began expressing doubt about whether or not she really needed to be there. She explained that she had made the appointment a few days after experiencing a setback during the New Year's holiday. In a surprised tone she reported that in the time between her call and the appointment she had somehow managed to "get back on track." She was, in other words, no longer drinking to the point where it was a problem.

Intrigued by the strength of her reported success, we decided to suspend our usual suspicion and disbelief long enough to investigate this positive turn of events. In response to our inquiries Blythe explained that she had been feeling rather low after the setback and thinking about how she would have to start treatment all over again when an idea suddenly occurred to her. The idea was to go back and review the notes she had kept about her treatment in her personal journal. Reviewing the notes, she told us, helped her recall how she had managed to overcome what was then a much more serious drinking problem. This, in turn, inspired her to implement that same approach again and ultimately resulted in her getting back on track.

As it turned out, we met with Blythe for only that one session. Given how she had dealt with the setback, we all agreed that additional treatment was not warranted. Today

Blythe continues to maintain the changes she had started making prior to that single visit. She is also, by the way, the head of her department at the school library.

❏

GAINING A NEW PERSPECTIVE ON CHANGE

Our experience with Blythe caused us to question our previous assumptions about setbacks and begin experimenting with new treatment methods. Soon a pattern began to emerge. Where we had once spent time trying to figure out what caused a setback and developing strategies to deal with that eventuality in the future, we now asked clients how they had managed to be successful in the past and encouraged them to engage in those activities again. Where we might have previously confronted clients and pointed out their weaknesses that led to lapses, we now focused on their obvious strengths and resources in getting back on course. Finally, for that remaining but increasingly small group of problem drinkers for which nothing else seemed to work, we experimented with a shotgun approach, exposing them to a variety of different approaches in the hope that some effective strategy might be found amid the diversity.

The results were dramatic. First and foremost, the problem drinkers were able to get back on track very quickly—most of the time within a single visit. Second, but equally important, the problem drinkers immediately began to feel better about themselves; this, in turn, seemed to empower them to confront future challenges and continue working hard to achieve their desired objectives. "If you constantly point out my failures," one of our clients once told us while reflecting on our approach, "I begin to feel like a failure. I start feeling that I can't do anything myself."

Our experimentation ultimately resulted in an entirely new perspective. This change in perspective is reflected in three simple rules of what we now call our central philosophy. In reality, these rules state not only our perspective regarding setbacks but also our philosophy about the nature of change in general.

RULE 1: IF IT AIN'T BROKE, DON'T FIX IT!

An occasional slip or setback does not necessarily mean that your strategy for solution is broken and requires fixing. As a species, however, we want to understand our experience—especially when it does not conform to our expectations. For this reason the temptation is great to stop, look around, and dissect and analyze the setbacks that we experience in the hope that such information will enable us to avoid future problems. Therapists and treatment professionals frequently oblige and even indulge this process by offering to investigate any of a variety of areas where the causes for our personal failures are popularly thought to be found—for example, in our parents, our childhood, our genes, disease, and our feelings.[4]

This preoccupation with failure and search for explanations in traditional approaches, however, miss the point. For one thing, like the now-proverbial traffic jam, there simply may be no good reason for the setback. As one of our colleagues is fond of saying, "Sometimes shit simply happens."[5] Valuable time may be wasted, therefore, searching for reasons that offer precious little in the way of solutions and may, by postponing more useful action, make matters worse.

Please don't misunderstand our point. Saying that there sometimes is no good reason for a setback is not the same as saying you will not be able to find a reason or reasons if you set your mind to it. Indeed, we are certain that you will be able to find a reason for your failure if you look long enough. Our question is, So what? There is no way to be certain that you have "discovered" the correct or "true" cause of the setback and, once it is discovered, no guarantee that knowing such information will prevent you from experiencing relapses in the future.

Consider an experience Scott had while growing up. In the California neighborhood where he was raised, there was a neighbor who was constantly borrowing tools and other gardening implements from Scott's father, Paul Miller, and then not returning them. The problem was solved one Sunday afternoon, when the man appeared at the front door, once again asking to borrow something—on this occasion, the lawn mower. Scott remembers the puzzled look on the man's face when his father told him that he could not borrow the lawn mower since the "family was having chicken for dinner this afternoon." It was true, Scott recalled, that the family was having chicken for dinner that afternoon. He had even driven with his father to the local Kentucky Fried Chicken outlet to buy the food. However, what that had to do with the neighbor's not being able to borrow the lawn mower was unclear in Scott's (and, more than likely, the neighbor's) mind. He thought about the incident for some time while munching on one of the Colonel's drumsticks. Unable to come up with a satisfactory answer, he finally broke down and asked his father what eating chicken had to do with lawn movers. His father quickly replied, "Scott, when you are looking for an excuse, one is as good as another."

Focusing on failure may also obscure the obvious: that the strategy you have been using may not be "broken" and may have, in fact, been working in large measure. After all, you cannot have a setback if you have not first experienced success. Indeed, by definition, experiencing a lapse means that you first must have been successful. Otherwise, how would you know that you had experienced a setback? Spending huge amounts of time analyzing setbacks and then trying to develop new strategies may cause you to miss this obvious fact. Moreover, spending time trying to develop a new strategy when the old one is not truly unworkable is tantamount to throwing the baby out with the bath water and may ultimately lead to the development of a hodgepodge of strategies that are, in total, less effective than the original.

Therefore, rather than try to find out what is broken and may have led to the setback, you should first respond to a relapse by simply *doing what was working before the setback occurred!* Remember Blythe, who, when experiencing a setback after a year of being successful, reviewed the notes she kept in her journal about the treatment and then implemented the same strategies that had helped her be successful before. She did not waste valuable time fretting over the cause of the setback. Nor did she dissect and analyze her method or attempt to locate the fault in her approach. Much to her credit, after overcoming the initial shock of the setback, she was wise enough to leave well enough alone and simply begin doing what had worked for her in the past.

Therefore, before you move on to the next section, we strongly advise you to take some time to reflect on your own experience. In particular, recall what you were doing to be successful prior to the setback even if the successes you experienced seem insignificant to you at the present moment. Don't let the shock and discouragement that invariably accompany personal setbacks dissuade you from giving serious consideration and merit to your successes—all your successes, however small or seemingly insignificant. After all, you can never know which success holds the key to lasting change. If you made written notes or kept a journal about your experience while you were reading this book, take some time to review those sources before moving on to the next rule.

RULE 2: ONCE YOU KNOW WHAT WORKS, *DO MORE OF IT.*

The surest way to be successful is to continue doing what makes you successful. As Alexander Dumas père said in volume one of *Ange Pitou*, "Nothing succeeds like success." Not infrequently, however, problem drinkers come to see us following a setback not recognizing that they have already managed to stop the problem and get back on track. Temporarily blinded by feelings

of failure, they overlook their hard work and dismiss the significance of their efforts in this process. But think about the situation for a moment. It is clear that the person has experienced a
setback. This is, however, only part of the picture and perhaps
not the most important part. By the time people have made it to
our office to talk about problem drinking episodes, they have already accomplished several things. First, they have recognized
there was a problem. Second, they have sought help. And third,
they have usually managed to stop or curtail the episode to some
degree. As we noted, however, it is easy to miss the significance
of these successes in the midst of feeling bad about the setback.

"What about the relapse?" some of you may ask. "Shouldn't
that be the focus of attention? Aren't we going to miss something important if we don't study our failures?" To these questions we answer, "Not right now." The most important matter is
getting back on track—back on the road to solution. Anything
else risks missing the forest for the trees. Temporary detours can
be frustrating and discouraging but should not be the focus of
attention. There will be plenty of time in the future to reflect on
such matters. For now, consider the following questions about
your success *after* the setback:

- **What . . .**
  . . . made you recognize that it was time to stop (or cut
  back)?
  . . . clues told you to stop when you did? How did you
  manage to pay attention to those clues? What are you
  doing to become more sensitive to these clues in the
  future?
  . . . was different about this setback from the last time?
  . . . exactly did you do differently this time (e.g., stop
  drinking earlier; have fewer drinks; drink in a different
  location, with different people, or a different type of
  alcohol; experience a different sequence of events)?
  . . . would others (spouse, friends, children employer) say
  was different this time?

... did you do to prevent this setback from becoming even
worse?

... do you know you must continue doing to ensure
success?

... minimally do you have to do to stay on track?

- **How . . .**

    ... did you finally manage to (stop or cut back on) your
    drinking when you did?

    ... would others (spouse, friends, children employer) say
    you managed to (stop or cut back on) your drinking when
    you did?

- **Who . . .**

    ... was with you when you decided to stop (or cut back
    on) your drinking? How did being with that person (or
    those persons) help?

    ... was not present when you decided to stop (or cut back
    on) your drinking that may have contributed to your
    decision? How did this person's or these persons' absence
    help you?

- **Where . . .**

    ... were you when you finally managed to gain some
    control once again? How did being there contribute to
    your being successful?

    ... did you go after the setback that helped you?

❑

IN AND OUT OF THE TOILET

Ronald had not had any problems with alcohol for nearly a year
when he experienced his first setback. It was a particularly bad
setback for Ronald. After a few weeks of problematic drinking,
however, he finally picked up the phone and made an
appointment to come in and see us. He was very discouraged
when he arrived for his scheduled appointment.

RONALD *(tearful):* I feel like such a failure. A whole year down the toilet.

THERAPIST: Sounds like you're feeling pretty down about this.

RONALD: You know it. I just can't get it out of my head. I just keep going over and over it. Why? Why? I keep asking myself.

TH: Let me ask you something. *How* did you manage to pull yourself out of the toilet long enough to pick up the phone and call?

RONALD: I just did it. I knew I needed help.

TH: *How* is that different from what you might have done in the past?

RONALD: Before, I wouldn't have called, I don't think. I would've just wallowed in it and kept drinking.

TH: You would have wallowed in it and kept drinking?

RONALD: Yeah.

TH: You say you would have kept drinking?

RONALD: Yeah.

TH: Does that mean you're not drinking now?

RONALD: I haven't had anything to drink for a couple of days now.

TH: Wow. *What* did you do to get yourself to stop like that?

RONALD: I just did it.

TH: You "just picked up the phone," you "just stopped drinking"? I don't believe it. You've been feeling really discouraged. It would have been really easy just to wallow around in it and keep drinking.

RONALD: I guess I didn't think about it like that, yeah.

TH: So *how* did you get yourself to stop like that? You must have done something.

RONALD *(thinking):* I took this case of beer that I had bought and I gave it to my neighbor.

TH: Uh-huh.

RONALD *(smiles and laughs):* I was gonna throw it away, but I just couldn't get myself to do that.

TH *(laughs):* Okay, you couldn't throw it away so . . .
RONALD: I gave it to my neighbor.

The discussion continued, with the therapist and Ronald working together to identify "what had worked" to help Ronald stop his problem drinking. Considerable time was spent helping him identify the who, what, where, when, and how of his success. As this discussion took place, Ronald's mood and outlook began to change. By the end of the session Ronald felt better about himself and, more important, had identified what he could do if another problem arose in the future.

One last point . . . before we move on to the next rule. There is one other way that people run into difficulty regarding Rule 2. Perhaps it is just human nature, but we have observed a tendency among problem drinkers to tinker with or change strategies that are working for them early in the change process. After experiencing some degree of success, you will likely be tempted to think that you no longer have to do everything you have been doing up to this point in order to continue being successful. We want to make you aware of this tendency and warn you that tampering with a successful strategy invites failure. The benefits of continuing to do what works is reflected in the popular saying "Don't change a winning ball game." To that we add this simple advice: Don't give into the temptation.

RULE 3: IF IT DOESN'T WORK, DON'T DO IT AGAIN; DO SOMETHING DIFFERENT.

Both of us happen to be bilingual. While our primary language is English, Insoo, a native of Korea, of course speaks Korean as well. Scott, having spent a number of years after high school living in Sweden, also speaks Swedish. Being able to speak the native languages of the people when we travel to these countries has afforded both of us an experience that nicely illustrates the third rule of the central philosophy. Whether one is at Arlanda International Airport just outside Stockholm, Sweden, or on the streets of Seoul, Korea, the experience is largely the same. You may have witnessed the same phenomenon or even had an experience similar to the one we are about to describe.

Usually the whole thing starts when a foreigner—typically an American—approaches a native to ask for something. Perhaps the American is trying to locate a tourist attraction in downtown Seoul, or maybe he just wants help completing the customs forms for entry into Sweden. Whatever the reason for the contact, a problem soon develops. In the typical scenario the American begins by explaining the predicament in which he finds himself. For example, he may begin by explaining—usually in English—how he is lost and how grateful he would be to receive some assistance in the way of directions. The native usually listens attentively, all the while nodding and smiling while the American speaks. When the American finally finishes, the native, who appears to the American to have listened and understood what he was saying, explains that he does not speak English. For example, the Swede may say to the American *in Swedish, "Jag talar inte engelska."* Hearing the person respond in his native tongue usually causes a perplexed look to creep across the American's face. Momentarily surprised, he may grow silent and even contemplative. It is apparent that the American is now considering what move to make next. The result, however, is usually the same: He will continue to try!

Speaking now at a much slower pace and being careful to enunciate each word, the American again states his request. "C o u l d   y o u "—emphasizing the "you" while simultaneously pointing to the native to add emphasis—" c o u l d y o u   *p l e a s e* . . . blah, blah, blah," to which the native once again responds (in his native tongue), *"J a g   t a l a r i n t e   e n g e l s k a* . . . *blahski, blahski, blahski."* The American usually shakes his head at this point, and both once again grow silent as they contemplate their next move.

As if the problem were that the native could not hear, the

American now shouts the request: "C O U L D   Y O U
H E L P   M E . . .   B L A H ,   B L A H ,   B L A H ." Perhaps
thinking the same thing about the American, however, the native quickly responds in kind: "J A G   T A L A R   I N T E   E N G E L -
S K A . . .   B L A H S K I ,   B L A H S K I ,   B L A H S K I !" The interaction usually escalates in this manner until one of the
participants gives up in disgust, invites someone else into the
conversation to help out, or engages in some other behavior that
is different from that which constituted the first interaction. In
other words, the problem continues and even worsens as long as
both participants insist on engaging in more of the same behavior. As you may have already surmised, the problem is solved
only when either one or both of the participants decide to stop
doing what is not working and do something different instead.
What exactly they do different is not the most important factor.
What is critical in terms of solving the problem is that they do
something, anything, different from what has not been working.

MILLER'S "FIRST LAW OF HOLES"

Scott is fond of referring to the principle behind Rule 3 as his
"First Law of Holes." Simply stated, the law is: "If you are in a
hole, stop digging!" Don't continue with a problem-solving strategy that is not working. You will only manage to become more
entrenched. This does not mean that following Rule 3 is easy.
While aware of the rule, we ourselves are frequently seduced
into thinking we can escape its application to us. In working with
a particular client, for example, we may become mired and
"stuck" in a hole made up of our determination to succeed with
a therapeutic strategy that is clearly not working. Temporarily
blinded by this determination, we administer a double, triple, or
quadruple dose of the same failed strategy to the client with the
sincere hope that such a measure will overcome the problem.

However, SHOUTING a failed method does little to solve the problem. In the end, you must abandon the failed method and do something different.

By the way, the importance of doing something different was underscored by the results of a small research study Scott and Larry Hopwood conducted some years ago. In the study we analyzed fifty cases that did not improve after receiving treatment. We wanted to know whether some inherent characteristics of these cases would allow us to predict beforehand if they would not benefit from our treatment. We started the study by examining a variety of factors, such as a person's diagnosis, the length and/or chronicity of the problem, the history of the family, and the motivation for treatment. We found little or no relationship between these factors and the eventual outcome of the case. In other words, none of these things seemed to predict whether or not a particular client ultimately benefited from the treatment. Surprised by these results, we then began to examine different aspects of the therapeutic encounter. Again we focused our efforts on the client. For example, we considered her participation in the interview, her answers to our questions, whether or not she followed through with our recommendations, etc. However, once again we found little or no relationship between these factors and the eventual outcome of the case.

Frustrated in our efforts to understand what accounted for the failure of some cases to respond to our method of treatment, we eventually decided to focus our attention on the only element that we had not considered previously: the therapist. And *voilà!* soon after turning our attention to the activities of the therapist, we discovered what we had been looking for all along. The characteristic that these cases shared was that the therapist employed the same treatment strategy from session to session despite the failure of that strategy to produce improvement in the client. In other words, failed cases resulted from a combination of the therapist and client's continuing to do the same damn thing over and over even though it was not working.

GETTING STUCK IN THE SAME DAMN THING

As we said earlier, it is easy to get seduced into repeating a failed problem-solving strategy. The hope we all have, of course, is that our persistence will pay off and we will eventually obtain the results we desire. Stuck with the grade school idea that effort should be rewarded on an equal footing with outcome, we continue to use a failed strategy. Far from funny, being stuck can easily lead to discouragement, which may ultimately result in giving up on trying to solve the problem. Like a bad dream in which we are pursued by a fire-breathing dragon, we continue with our futile efforts, such as trying to run away or fight the dragon, when the only real solution is to wake up[6] when the only real solution is, in other words, to do something that is truly different.

One of the primary publications of traditional treatment, the so-called *Big Book* of Alcoholics Anonymous, boldly asserts: "Rarely have we seen a person fail who has thoroughly followed our path. Those who do not recover are people who cannot or will not completely give themselves to this simple program, usually men and women who are constitutionally incapable of being honest with themselves. . . . They are naturally incapable of grasping and developing a manner of living which demands rigorous honesty."[7] This brief excerpt from the book is usually used to explain why some people fail to respond to Alcoholics Anonymous. We could not possibly disagree with this explanation more. As we indicated in the opening chapters of this book, there is no one way for a person to solve a drinking problem. The phenomenon is complex and defies a simple, one-size-fits-all solution. Each person must find and develop his or her own solution. That is what the "miracle" method is all about.

Further, our experience and research have shown us that the best way to deal with treatment failures is *not* to blame the person seeking help but rather to quickly seek and initiate alternative methods for approaching an individual's problems with alcohol. Please don't misunderstand our point. We readily acknowledge that people have responded and do respond to the traditional approach of Alcoholics Anonymous. Indeed, we have witnessed the positive effects of this approach with some of our own clients. We have also observed, however, a strong tendency—obvious in the above quote from *The Big Book*—always to attribute treatment failures to the person in need of help rather than to the method of treatment. If you happen to find yourself in the position of accepting blame for a treatment method, strategy, or program that has not helped you obtain the results you desire, you should reevaluate that position. Rather than spend precious time analyzing what is wrong with *you*, it is probably time for you to investigate other options and *try something different*.

By the way, the same holds true for the method espoused in this book. As we indicated at the beginning of the book, we have no illusions about having discovered the one true, correct, or even best way for helping people solve their problems with alcohol. Rather, our hope has been to add to the increasingly diverse number of treatment options available to people who want to bring an end to their problem drinking.

HOW TO FIND SOMETHING DIFFERENT TO DO

The following questions are intended to help you generate some ideas about things you can do differently when you find yourself stuck in the position of doing more of the same damn thing. Please be aware, however, that these questions do not represent an exhaustive list of options available but are simply those to which our clients have responded most frequently.

ARE YOU TRYING TOO HARD?

Believe it or not, it is possible to work *too* hard in trying to solve a personal problem. This seems to be particularly true of people trying to bring about changes in their drinking. While the traditional approach paints a picture of problem drinkers as "resistant" and "in denial," our own experience in treating problem drinkers for the last twenty years has led us to a very different perspective. Far from lacking motivation, our problem drinking clients often suffer from having too much determination to change. We sometimes say that they are "victims of their own enthusiasm." Hoping, perhaps, to repair damaged relationships or to increase deflated senses of self-esteem, they set ridiculously high goals and hold themselves to impossible standards. Not recognizing that the standards and goals they set are impossible from the outset, they subject themselves to a barrage of self-criticism and guilt after failing to succeed. The result, not surprisingly, is often a relapse into drinking.

For this reason we sometimes ask clients who are experiencing difficulty if they might be working too hard, if they are, in other words, asking too much of themselves too early in the process of change. Have they set their standards for success too high? Are they ignoring evidence of small changes in their behavior because they are overly focused on obtaining a large result? Would they notice a small but significant change if it did happen? What would constitute a small but significant change? What is the minimal change they would be satisfied with at this time?

On occasion our clients argue with us when we ask them these questions. They insist, for example, that we are "going easy on them" or "setting our standards too low." Explaining the reason for the questions usually has no effect on their determination. Perhaps they are, in a manner of speaking, *resistant*—that is, resistant to changing at a more reasonable pace!

The point is that it is entirely possible to work too hard. If you suspect this to be true of your own situation, one of the first things you can do is reevaluate your goals and standards. Begin by asking yourself how you would know if you made just a small amount of change in your current situation. You may find one of the scaling-type questions we presented in the last chapter useful in this process. For example, on a scale from 1 to 10, if you rate your current status as a 1, try to describe what will be different when you have moved from that position to a 1.25 or 1.50. We know this will be difficult for those of you who are "chronically overmotivated." However, setting more realistic goals and standards and defining small signs of progress is the first step in getting back on the road to solution.

Do You Need to Take a Vacation from Change?

If the first suggestion doesn't seem to fit for you, then you may want to consider taking a brief vacation from change. That's right—a vacation from your efforts to solve your drinking problem. The idea behind this suggestion is simple. Just like a real-life vacation, you may want to take a break from trying to change. Taking such a break allows you to get some distance from your present situation, in particular, your current problem-solving efforts. In turn this distance can help you gain a new perspective on your situation that may suggest new problem-solving alternatives. We usually recommend a vacation of at least one or two weeks. However long you decide to take, once you have made a decision, be sure to take the *entire* vacation. If you are like other people, new ideas will begin flowing shortly after beginning your therapy vacation. Don't give in to the temptation to return to work early. Take your time, jot down the ideas and alternatives as they occur to you, and start implementing them only at the conclusion of your time off.

Is Your Miracle Clear?

In other words, do you know what you want? What your treatment objective is? Or whether you would know if you had attained your objective? How about if you were only getting part of what you had hoped for? Would you notice the changes then? What would those changes be? Do the changes you are looking for have the qualities of the six keys for success presented in Chapter 3? (Do you even remember what the six keys for success are?)

If you can't remember the six keys, then it is entirely possible that the goals you have set for yourself may be preventing you from experiencing the success you desire rather than enabling you to achieve it. In fact, working on goals that do not have the six qualities of success is one of the most common reasons for failure that we observe in the treatment of problem drinkers. For this reason one of the first things we do when a client experiences difficulty in changing problem drinking is to determine whether or not the client's goals have these six qualities. Recall that the six keys for success are:

- Make sure your miracle is important to you.
- Keep it small.
- Make it specific, concrete, and behavioral.
- Be sure you state what you will do rather than what you won't do.
- State how you will start your journey rather than how you will end it.
- Be clear about who, what, where, and when, but not why.

If you have forgotten your six keys, take time now to review your treatment objectives—in other words, your miracle picture. Does your miracle have the six keys? Even if you believe that your goals reflect these qualities, you may find it useful to reread Chapter 3 and answer all the questions again. If you didn't do so before, you should write down your responses to the questions this time.

ARE YOU A CUSTOMER FOR CHANGE? A COMPLAINANT? A VISITOR?

As you have been reading this book, have you taken the time to answer all the questions? Do the exercises? Try out the recommendations? Have you kept notes? Charted your progress? Kept notes about your strategies for success? Made charts? If the answer to these questions is an unequivocal "Yes!," you are probably what we call a customer for change. You are, in other words, the type of person who recognizes that there is a problem and knows that the solution requires you to take some action.

If, however, you have read this book without taking the time to answer the questions, do the exercises, or try any of the homework tasks, you are probably not a customer for change. You are likely what we refer to as a complainant. Complainants are people who are not willing to extend anything more than the most minimal effort in attempting to solve a problem. They hope to change through what we jokingly refer to as "bibliosmosis"—somehow absorbing the ideas in a book without any effort on their part. Complainants often believe that someone else has the problem and, therefore, should be required to change first—for example, their spouses, their employers, probation officers, or even their therapists. All the while they may say they want things to change. They complain loudly and consistently about their problems. However, they often wait for change to happen to them rather than make change happen for them.

What can you do if you suspect you are a complainant rather than a customer for change? For one thing, you can hope and pray that your situation improves without your participation. However, the reality is, as we have repeatedly pointed out in the book, that few people change solely through their reading of a book. Even if you add hope and prayer to your reading, your chances for success are far more limited than if you can actually get yourself to *do* something. Change requires *your* action.

Perhaps the most important question, then, is how to increase your motivation to act on changing your behavior. Recognizing that you are a complainant rather than a customer is probably the first step. People often mistake themselves for customers because they think that complaining about a problem or nagging someone else to change is the action in which they need to engage in order to bring about a solution. But this is the behavior of a complainant, not a customer. You may have to wait for a long time if all you do is complain or if you insist that others change before you do. Moreover, while you wait, the problem may worsen and your suffering may increase. While it would be nice if others changed first, the reality is that your own efforts and actions are the only real guarantee of change.

The second step is deciding what to change about yourself or your situation. Following the process we outlined in Chapter 3 can be helpful in this respect. Include only those things that you *can* change, and for now let everything else go. The simple truth is that you are more likely to feel motivated about working on something that is of interest to you and that you have the power to change.

If you believe you have no problem with alcohol and are reading the book only because someone has forced you to, then you are neither a customer nor a complainant. Rather, you are most likely what we refer to as a visitor. Not infrequently, visitors have been forced to seek professional services by the courts, spouses, or employers but do not believe that they have a problem. They may just be biding their time until they no longer have to participate in a certain program or type of treatment.

The question, of course, is what you can do if you find yourself in the position of the visitor. Perhaps you really don't have a problem. Maybe you do stand unjustly accused or unfairly sentenced to a program that does not fit your needs. What can you do then? Of course, time will pass. Whoever is accusing you of having a problem *may* eventually forget about it. You *may* eventually be released from your obligation to the person, court, or treatment program that holds you captive. If you choose, you can simply bide your time until something else happens.

Or you can use the time available to work on something that is of interest to you personally. In this fast-paced world we rarely have the opportunity to slow down long enough to think about what we want out of life, much less to direct our efforts toward achieving it. Perhaps the time you have can be used to do exactly that: to think about what you want and devise a plan to obtain it. Taking some action will at least give the appearance that you are working on something; this in turn might get the person or persons who are complaining about you off your back. With some minor variations the method described in this book can be useful in helping you achieve goals that are not directly related to overcoming the problem drinking. Give it some consideration. What have you got to lose?

ARE YOU TOO CONFIDENT?

As we said earlier, problems drinkers are sometimes the "victims" of their own determination to succeed. This not only results in their setting unreachable goals and having impossibly high standards but frequently causes them to underestimate the chances of experiencing a relapse or setback along the road to solution. Underestimating also causes them to underprepare for the inevitable setbacks that characterize the change process.

This would not be a problem if overconfident problem drinkers somehow managed to learn from experience. Such learning might be evidenced, for example, by problem drinkers' setting smaller, more realistic goals or making more realistic evaluations about their chances for future relapse and preparing for that eventuality. Frequently, however, experiencing a setback leads to the opposite behavior. Faced with failure, overconfident problem drinkers often redouble their efforts to succeed and set even higher goals and standards for themselves. The new efforts and higher standards lead to a false sense of security, which once again leads to underestimating and underpreparing for future setbacks. The result is a cycle of escalating effort, constantly renewed vows and promises to change, and chronic relapsing.

What can you do if this is happening to you? Simply stop underestimating the chances of experiencing future setbacks, and take some time now to prepare adequately for that possibility. You can begin by thinking about the setbacks you have already experienced and then developing a plan for avoiding the situations and circumstances that place you at increased risk. You may find these questions helpful:

- **What . . .**
  . . . do I know I can do to increase the risk of experiencing a setback? What else? What can I do now to decrease the risk?
  . . . am I usually doing immediately before a setback that may cause it to occur? What can I do instead?
  . . . would others say I do immediately before a setback that causes it to occur? What would they say I should do instead?
  . . . thoughts, feelings, and behaviors occur immediately before a setback that may cause it to occur? Would others (e.g., spouse, family member, friend, employer) agree?
  . . . thoughts, feelings, and behaviors would others say occur immediately before a setback that may cause it to occur? What thoughts, feelings, and behaviors would they say I should replace them with?
- **Where . . .**
  . . . am I most likely to be when I experience a setback (e.g., at home, a bar, during a certain event)? Where can I go instead that would decrease the risk of a setback?
  . . . would others (e.g., spouse, family member, friend, employer) say I am most likely to be when I am most likely to experience a setback? Where would they say I should go instead?
- **Who . . .**
  . . . is most likely to be with me when I experience a setback (e.g., certain friends or acquaintances, family

members)? Whom should I definitely avoid? Whom should I be with instead?

. . . would others (e.g., spouse, family member, friend, employer) say is most likely to be with me when I experience a setback? Whom would they say I should definitely avoid? Whom would they suggest I be with instead?

- **When . . .**

. . . am I most likely to experience a setback? What time of day? What day of the week? What can I do differently in the future to decrease this risk?

. . . would others (e.g., spouse, family member, friend, employer) say I am most likely to experience a setback? What time of day? What day of the week? What would they say I can do differently in the future to decrease this risk?

IS THERE ANYTHING ELSE YOU CAN THINK OF TO DO DIFFERENTLY?

Clearly the questions and recommendations up to this point do not represent an exhaustive list of options available to the person having difficulty in changing his or her behavior. We have included only those ideas that have proved useful to the broad range of problem drinkers with whom we have worked over the years. In reality the list of options is limitless. After digging yourself deeply enough into a hole, however, we understand that it can be difficult to see any options other than simply continuing to dig. It is easy to get caught in the trap of repeating more of the same damn thing that doesn't work.

Since you now know, however, that continuing to use the same old strategy is guaranteed to fail, it is crucial to figure out what you can do differently now that might increase the chances of success in the future. Anything you do that is somehow different from your current approach stands a better chance of succeeding. You know that your present approach to the problem does not work. Continuing to use this same strategy will, therefore, guarantee failure. For this reason you need to consider other actions and approaches available to you.

Take some time to brainstorm the possible alternatives now. If you've never tried brainstorming before, here is how it is done. First, find a pleasant, quiet place where you will be able to sit undisturbed for about ten minutes. Then, with paper and pencil in hand, begin considering things you could do differently to solve your problem. Allow your mind to wander and your imagination complete freedom to consider any and all alternatives—however unrealistic or crazy they may seem to you at the time. Don't evaluate, be critical, or censure any ideas. For ten minutes or so just let your mind be free to consider all the possibilities. However, be sure to jot down the ideas as they occur to you. Afterward review the list you generated, and determine which, if any, of the items you might want to try. Don't be surprised if it takes you several times to start generating options that you think will get you moving again or have an impact on your situation.

In addition to or in combination with brainstorming, you may find the following exercise helpful. We call it the garbage list exercise. It begins with making a list of all the things you are presently doing to solve your problem that you know do not work. Be sure that your list is exhaustive—that it contains everything you have tried that has not worked—and leave those items off your list that work either occasionally or under certain circumstances or conditions. The only items on the list should be the ones you know to be *un*successful in helping you solve your drinking problem.

After making your list, carefully review each item. Then make a solemn promise to yourself that you will not engage in any of the unsuccessful attempted solutions contained on your list. Instead, commit yourself to do something different. You need not know what that something will be at the time you make the commitment. Simply make a promise to yourself to do something different.

Do You Need Outside Help?

If you have tried the ideas suggested up to this point without success, it may be time to consider seeking professional assistance. While the research indicates that self-help books are more helpful to readers than previously thought, it is clear that not everyone can receive the help he or she needs from a book.[8] Sometimes additional help is required in the form of treatment with a mental health care professional.

Treatment need not necessarily be long-term or expensive. As we indicated at the beginning of this book, advances in the technique and practice of therapy are allowing treatment professionals to help clients much more quickly than was previously thought possible. While the rate of change varies some for each therapist and client, you should begin seeing change within weeks rather than within months or years. Of course, this does not mean that all your problems will be resolved overnight. It does mean, however, that you should expect to see some results from the therapy within the first four or five visits and definitely by the tenth visit. If no results are forthcoming, you should talk about it with your therapist. Steer clear of treatment professionals who say that treatment and recovery are necessarily a lifelong process.

With regard to cost, most insurance companies provide coverage for at least part of the cost associated with visits to a mental health care professional. Check your policy or talk with an insurance agent to determine the benefits available to you. Most such contacts are confidential, and you need not go into detail about the nature of your problem in order to find out about the coverage your policy provides.

There are also several options for those who do not have insurance coverage. Most communities, for example, have mental health centers that offer services to the public at little or no charge. Contrary to what some people believe, such agencies are often in the forefront of mental health treatment and provide excellent, up-to-date clinical services. Usually the number for community mental health agencies can be obtained from the phone book in the section for local government.

Another option is to contact treatment professionals directly and talk to them about the cost of their services. In particular, you may want to ask if the professional charges on what is called a sliding scale. This refers to the clinician's willingness to negotiate a fee for treatment services that is dependent on your income and ability to pay. The rate for clinical services varies greatly among professionals, corresponding roughly to the amount and type of training they have as well as their geographic locations. In general, fees are higher across all professional groups on the East and West coasts and in large metropolitan areas. Typically, psychiatrists have the highest fees, followed somewhat in descending order by psychologists, social workers, marriage and family therapists, professional counselors, and certified drug and alcohol counselors. You should be aware, however, that there is great variability in the cost of professional services and that a higher fee does not necessarily guarantee a better outcome or even better treatment services.

Professionals who are unwilling to talk openly and directly about their fees are probably best avoided. We have heard, for example, of some unscrupulous professionals who have told potential clients that their concern about the cost of services actually reflects their underlying denial of the problem or their ambivalence toward seeking treatment. Nothing could be further from the truth. If anything, seeking information about the cost of services reflects your underlying sense of responsibility and desire to establish an open, honest working relationship with a treatment professional.

Just as fees vary greatly from one professional to the next, so do the quality and nature of the services they offer. What matters most is finding a counselor who "fits" with you and your experience and who is flexible and skilled enough to try a variety of approaches in helping you solve your problem. Beware of those professionals insisting on a one-size-fits-all treatment package.

What is the best way to find a good therapist? Friends, relatives, neighbors, or representatives of your clergy are frequently good sources to consult. Someone who has had a positive and productive experience with a specific therapist is often the most reliable source for a recommendation. Whatever the source of the referral, however, we recommend that you interview several potential candidates prior to making a selection.

In choosing a professional to help you with your drinking problem, you may have heard that it is best to seek counseling from a counselor who has been successful in overcoming his or her own problems with alcohol. Proponents of traditional approaches, for example, argue that treatment professionals who have experienced and overcome their own problems with alcohol make better counselors and achieve better outcomes with problem drinkers. While the argument has a certain amount of commonsense appeal, the research on the topic clearly indicates that the recovery status of the helping professional does not contribute to better treatment outcomes.[9] Moreover, the apparent logic of the argument—that like begets like and therefore, like should treat like—falls apart when it is scrutinized carefully. How far, for example, should the argument extended? Should depressed people be treated only by counselors who have themselves been clinically depressed? Schizophrenic people be treated only by former schizophrenics? Should we prohibit family doctors from treating illnesses they have not experienced? The argument quickly reaches the level of the absurd. As Lou Grant from the "Mary Tyler Moore Show" once said, "You don't have to be a whale to write *Moby Dick*." Therefore, working with a therapist who also happens to be a former problem drinker is ultimately a matter of personal choice. Once again, the critical issue is whether the counselor "fits" with you and your experience.

THE MIRACLE METHOD
READY REFERENCE
❑

THREE RULES FOR DEALING
WITH SETBACKS

1. If it ain't broke, don't fix it.
2. Once you know what works, do more of it.
3. If it doesn't work, don't do it again; do something different.

Epilogue

ON THE NATURE OF MIRACLES

> No testimony for any kind of miracle has ever
> amounted to a proof . . . it is experience only.
> —David Hume, *Enquiries*

There is an ancient story of two apprentice Zen monks who are discussing their respective masters while cleaning their temple. Proud to be the student of such a famous monk, the first novice tells his companion about the many miracles that he has seen his master perform. "I have watched," the young novice says, "as my master has turned an entire village of people to the Buddha, has made rain fall from a dry sky, and has caused the mountains move!"

The other novice listens attentively and then, demonstrating his clear understanding of Zen, responds, "My master also does many miraculous things. When he is hungry, he eats. When he is thirsty, he drinks. When he is tired, he sleeps."

The story of these two Zen novices reflects our conflicting thoughts and feelings as we come to the conclusion of this book. While we would like it very much if the method described in the book helps create a miracle in your life, we recognize, like the second novice, that such occurrences do not represent what is really important in life. What is truly important is your being able to experience fully all the pleasures and pains of normal, everyday living, free from the problems caused by alcohol, going to work, raising a family, making a home, paying the bills, and so on.

Like this book, all treatment contact must end. This is the way it should be. Treatment professionals meet with clients for a purpose. That purpose is to help the client return to normal life as quickly and efficiently as possible. If reading this book has helped you in this regard, then we have accomplished our objective. We wish you luck on the rest of your journey toward solution.

Notes

PREFACE

1. V. E. Johnson (1986), *Intervention: How to Help Someone Who Doesn't Want Help* (Minneapolis: Johnson Institute Books), pp. 6–7.
2. Ibid., p. 7.
3. Alcoholics Anonymous (1976), *Alcoholics Anonymous: The Story of How Thousands of Men and Women Have Recovered from Alcoholism.* (New York: Alcoholics Anonymous World Services, Inc.). Known as *The Big Book.*

CHAPTER 2: THERAPIST-DEPENDENT NO MORE!

1. E. Kristol (June 1990), Declarations of Codependence, *American Spectator.*
2. H. Gravitz and J. Bowden (1987), *Recovery: A Guide for Adult Children of Alcoholics* (New York: Simon and Schuster), preface.
3. S. Peele (1989), *The Diseasing of America: Addiction Treatment out of Control* (Lexington, Mass.: Lexington Books).
4. Cf H. J. Shaffer and S. B. Jones (1989), *Quitting Cocaine: The Struggle against Impulse* (Lexington, Mass.: Lexington Books) See also S. J. Wolin and S. Wolin (1993). *The Resilient Self: How Survivors of Troubled Families Rise above Adversity* (New York: Villard Books).
5. P. Watzlawick (1987), "If You Desire to See, Learn How to Act." In *Evolution of Psychotherapy,* ed. J. Zeig (New York: Brunner-Mazel), p. 93.
6. L. Robbins (1979), "Addict Careers." In *Handbook on Drug Abuse,* ed. R. Dupont, A. Goldstein, and J. O'Donnell (Rockville, Md.: National Institute on Drug Abuse). p. 332.

7. S. J. Wolin (January/February, 1992), "How to Survive Practically Anything," *Psychology Today*, 25(1), pp. 36–39.

8. Wolin, and Wolin op. cit.,

9. V. E. Johnson (1973), *I'll Quit Tomorrow* (New York: Harper and Row), p. 4.

10. S. Peele (1985), *The Meaning of Addiction: Compulsive Experience and Its Interpretation* (Lexington, Mass.: Lexington Books).

11. Johnson, op. cit., p. 1.

12. Ibid.

13. In his book *Putting Difference to Work* ([1992] New York: W. W. Norton), Steve de Shazer, cites the average number of sessions as 4.7.

14. I. K. Berg and L. Hopwood (1992), "Doing with Very Little: Brief Treatment of the Homeless Substance Abuser, *Journal of Independent Social Work*, 5(3–4), pp. 109–20.

15. *The Alcoholism Report: The Authoritative Newsletter for Professionals in the Field of Alcoholism* (1990), p. 1.

16. V. E. Johnson (1986), *Intervention: How to Help Someone Who Doesn't Want Help* (Minneapolis: Johnson Institute Books), p. ix.

17. S. D. Miller (1992), "The Symptoms of Solution," *Journal of Strategic and Systemic Therapies*, 11(1), pp. 1–11.

18. S. Coontz (1992), *The Way We Never Where: American Families and the Nostalgia Trap* (New York: Basic Books).

19. G. Marlatt, B. Deming, and J. B. Reid (1973), "Loss of Control Drinking in Alcoholics: An Experimental Analogue," *Journal of Abnormal Psychology*, 81, pp. 233–41.

20. Cited in S. Friedman (1993), *The New Language of Change: Constructive Collaboration in Psychotherapy* (New York: Guilford).

21. Wolin and Wolin, op. cit., p. 18.

22. David B. Reiser, M.D., personal communication, 1984.

23. C.f. B. L. Weiss (1988), *Many Lives, Many Masters: The True Story of a Prominent Psychiatrist, His Young Patient, and the Past-Life Therapy That Changed Both Their Lives* (New York: Simon and Schuster).

24. Jay Haley, cited in W. H. O'Hanlon and J. Wilk (1987), *Shifting Contexts: The Generation of Effective Psychotherapy* (New York: Guilford).

CHAPTER 3: UNLOCKING THE DOOR TO SOLUTION

1. W. R. Miller (1987), "Motivation and Treatment Goals," *Drugs and Society, 1*, pp. 133–51.
   See also M. W. Parker, D. K. Winstead, and F. J. P. Willi (1979), "Patient Autonomy in Alcohol Rehabilitation: 1. Literature Review," *International Journal of the Addictions, 14*, pp. 1015–22.
2. W. R. Miller, R. G. Benefield, and J. S. Tonigan (1993), "Enhancing Motivation for Change: A Controlled Comparison of Two Styles," *Journal of Consulting and Clinical Psychology, 61*(3), pp. 455–61.
3. Alcoholics Anonymous (1955), *Alcoholics Anonymous: The Story of How Many Thousands of Men and Women Have Recovered from Alcoholism,* (2d ed.) (New York: Alcoholics Anonymous World Services, Inc.), p. 95.
4. The therapist in this case was Larry Hopwood, Ph.D., M.S.W., the executive director of Problems to Solutions, Inc., Milwaukee, Wisconsin.
5. J. Orford and G. Edwards (1977), *Alcoholism—A Comparison of Treatment and Advice, with a Study of the Influence of Marriage* (Oxford: Oxford University Press).
6. V. E. Johnson (1986), *Intervention: How to Help Someone Who Doesn't Want Help* (Minneapolis: Johnson Institute Books), pp. 8–9.
7. Personal communication, 1986.
8. David Hawkins, personal communication, 1991.
9. Johnson, op. cit., p. 55.

CHAPTER 4: LESSONS FROM OZ

1. Alcoholics Anonymous (1976). *Alcoholics Anonymous* (3rd ed.). New York: Alcoholics Anonymous World Services, p. 59.
2. V. Johnson (1986), *Intervention: How to Help Someone Who Doesn't Want Help* (Minneapolis: Johnson Institute Books), pp. 6–7.
3. B. L. Duncan and D. W. Moynihan (1994). "Applying Outcome

Research: Intentional Utilization of the Client's Frame of Reference." *Psychotherapy*, *31*(2), pp. 294–301.

S. Garfield and A. E. Bergin (1986), *Handbook of Psychotherapy and Behavior Change*, 3d ed. (New York: John Wiley and Sons).

4. Scott D. Miller (1993, 1994), "From Problem to Solution: The Solution-Focused Brief Therapy Approach," *Brief Therapy Training Handouts* (Chicago: Author).
5. Sir Arthur Conan Doyle (1988), "Silver Blaze," *The Memoirs of Sherlock Holmes* (Pleasantville, N.Y. Reader's Digest Association, Inc.), pp. 11–35.
6. R. Nisbett and L. Ross (1980), *Human Inference: Strategies and Shortcomings of Social Judgment* (Englewood Cliffs, N.J.: Prentice-Hall).
7. M. Weiner-Davis, S. de Shazer, and W. Gingerich (1987), "Building on Pre-treatment Change to Construct the Therapeutic Solution: An Exploratory Study, *Journal of Marital and Family Therapy*, *13*(4), pp. 359–64.
8. Johnson, op. cit.
9. Cf H. J. Shaffer and S. B. Jones (1989), *Quitting Cocaine: The Struggle against Impulse* (Lexington, Mass.: Lexington Books).
10. Weiner-Davis, de Shazer, Gingerich, op. cit., p. 360.

CHAPTER 5: MAKING YOUR DREAM A REALITY

1. Some years later Scott learned that his father had arranged the "chance" meeting with magician. Scott's father, a school principal, had met the magician at a performance he gave at his elementary school.
2. E. Lorenz (1963), "Deterministic Non-periodic Flow," *Journal of the Atmospheric Sciences*, 20, pp. 130–41.
3. H. Spiegel and L. Linn (1969), "The Ripple Effect" Following Adjunct Hypnosis in Analytic Psychotherapy, *American Journal of Psychiatry*, 126, pp. 53–58.
4. E. Rossi (1973), "Psychological Shocks and Creative Moments in Psychotherapy," *American Journal of Clinical Hypnosis*, 16 (1), p. 14.

CHAPTER 6: HELP! I'VE FALLEN AND I CAN'T GET UP

1. D. Feldman (1987), *Imponderables: The Solution to the Mysteries of Everyday Life* (New York: Morrow), pp. 25–26.
2. I. K. Berg and S. D. Miller (1992), *Working with the Problem Drinker: A Solution-Focused Approach* (New York: W. W. Norton).
3. Ibid., pp. 16–17.
4. C. Sykes (1993), *A Nation of Victims* (New York: St. Martin's Press).
5. S. de Shazer (1991), "Shit happens." In *Strange Encounters with Carl Auer,* ed. G. Weber and F. Simon (New York: W. W. Norton), pp. 99–101.
6. P. Watzlawick, J. Weakland, and R. Fisch (1974), *Change: Principles of Problem Formation and Problem Resolution* (New York: W. W. Norton).
7. Alcoholics Anonymous (1976), *Alcoholics Anonymous: The Story of How Many Thousands of Men and Women Have Recovered from Alcoholism* (New York: Alcoholics Anonymous World Services, Inc.), p. 58.
8. R. A, Gould, and G. A. Clum (1993), "A Meta-analysis of Self-help Treatment Approaches," *Clinical Psychology Review,* 13(2), pp. 169–86.
9. Institute of Medicine (1990), *Broadening the Base of Treatment for Alcohol Problems* (Washington, D.C.: National Academy Press).

Index

❏

For information about
professional training opportunities
in the miracle method, please write:

Scott Miller, Ph.D.
Brief Therapy Network
P.O. Box 578264
Chicago, IL 60657-8264

or

Insoo Kim Berg
Brief Therapy Center
13965 W. Burleigh St.
Milwaukee, WI 53213-0736

❏